EssaySnark's Strategies for the
2014-'15 MBA Application for
DUKE FUQUA

# EssaySnark's Strategies for the 2014-'15 MBA Application for DUKE FUQUA

by EssaySnark®

Snarkolicious Press

Paperback edition
first published August 11, 2013
2014 version published July 6, 2014

Snarkolicious Press
P. O. Box 50021
Palo Alto, CA 94303

www.snarkoliciouspress.com

978 1 938098 27 7

© 2013-2014 by EssaySnark®

Cover image © Eric Isselée, used under license from Fotolia.com

All rights reserved. EssaySnark is a registered trademark. No part of this book may be reproduced or transmitted in any form or by any means, electronic or mechanical, including photocopying, recording, transcribing, or by an information storage system, without permission from the publisher. Essay questions reproduced within are copyright Fuqua School of Business.

This publication is provided "as is", without warranty of any kind, either express or implied. The author and Snarkolicious Press assume no liability for errors or omissions in this publication or other documents which are referenced or linked to this publication. While we certainly hope that you will be successful in your quest for admission to an MBA program, we cannot offer any promises that you will be, whether or not you adopt the advice provided herein. In no event shall Snarkolicious Press or its authors, principals, subsidiaries, partners, or owners be liable for any special, incidental, indirect or consequential damages of any kind, or any damages whatsoever, arising out of or in conjunction with the use or performance of this information. Applicants to any graduate program or university should verify the school's policies, application requirements, processes, procedures, and other criteria. This publication could include technical or other inaccuracies or typographical errors. Changes are periodically added to the information herein; these changes will be incorporated into new editions of this publication. Thus, different versions or formats of this publication may include different information.

Look for other *SnarkStrategies Guides* (digital and paperback) at your favorite bookseller or on the EssaySnark blahg at http://essaysnark.com.

FOLLOW ESSAYSNARK ON TWITTER!

"A goal without a plan is just a wish."

*Antoine de Saint-Exupéry*

## Duke's Application Is a BSer Favorite

Duke won EssaySnark's poll of best essay questions two years in a row, and they got rated as one of the top schools for "getting to know" their applicants by another admissions industry survey in Spring 2014. Brave Supplicants typically come away from the Duke application process feeling like they've been heard. Somehow, when you know that you had a chance to share yourself with the adcom, it feels a little bit better if they still end up rejecting you. With a school like HBS and its very impersonal process, a rejection often accompanies this feeling that they didn't even try to understand who you are.

Duke rolled these questions out in the 2012-2013 application season and lucky for you, they've kept them largely the same this year. They did introduce an alternative prompt for the second essay, which offers some flexibility – or complication, depending on how you look at it. We dissect the pros and cons of each prompt so that you can make an informed, strategic decision on which to tackle.

We were quite pleased when we heard that the app would stay the same. The questions are straightforward. They're easy to understand. The adcom is not trying to trick you – not intentionally at least, though there are some sticky bits with the new Essay 2 option. But it's not like Duke is out to get you; instead, they're on your side. Not like it seems some other schools are...

Here's what one person said about the Duke essays in our end-of-season survey:

> *Duke's 25 random gave me the opportunity to really express my personality, and their second essay gave ample room to express fit.*

And another:

> *Duke allowed me tons of leeway (and space) to include lots of different info, which helped me paint a more complete picture of myself.*

The challenge for you will be to write the second essay (friends and family) with the right tone, and the right detail, or if you choose the new alternate prompt, to dig in deep enough with the Fuqua Principles and to write in a non-stilted way. And, you will undoubtedly have trouble corralling your future plans into the very confined space required of the short-answer questions about career goals.

This *SnarkStrategies Guide* points you in the right direction for all of these issues. We also discuss the different interview policies at Duke and give some advice on how to manage that process. There's a section for reapplicants, in case you're in that boat – and if you are, your prospects are strong. Duke is exceptionally friendly to reapplicants.

Before we get too far: Please don't mistake Duke for a "safety school." Besides the fact that we dislike that term – it's so insulting to the school – we also caution you against a sense of complacency when it comes to the schools that don't have that brand name cachet. Duke is a very respected school both in the U.S. and overseas. They have a lower average GMAT score and their yield is somewhat lower, which indicates that they are not everyone's first choice – however for people who do their homework and understand what they're about, Duke often becomes a very attractive MBA target. You cannot slap together a set of essays for Duke and assume that you'll get in on a strong GMAT alone. One reason that their GMAT may be a little lower is because they actually pass up apps from very high-scoring applicants at times, when they can tell there's no appropriate fit. Don't make that mistake.

The Duke essays will be a lot of work and it would be a shame to make any assumptions about how easy it might be to get in. But you will have some fun in figuring out how to deal with them!

# Table of Contents

What to Know About Duke?...............................................................................1
What Is Duke Known For?................................................................................5
    What you won't get here.............................................................................7
What's Important at Duke..................................................................................9
The Interview and Your Duke Application Strategy.......................................11
    Open Interview............................................................................................11
    Everyone should interview on campus.......................................................14
Duke and Early Action.....................................................................................17
    Duke and other rounds...............................................................................20
Duke and Debt.................................................................................................22
Your Duke Strategy..........................................................................................24
    One more comment on the Duke application ..........................................25
Duke Evaluation Criteria.................................................................................27
    GMAT..........................................................................................................27
    Grades.........................................................................................................28
    Older Applicant..........................................................................................28
Reapplying to Duke.........................................................................................29
Your Duke Essays.............................................................................................33
    Your Duke Career Goals............................................................................34
    EssaySnark's career goals exercise.............................................................34
Duke Short-Answer Questions.......................................................................43
    Constructing Your Short-Answer Responses...........................................43
Essay 1: 25 Random Things............................................................................47
Essay 2: Why Duke?.........................................................................................49
    Duke Second Essay Prompt #1..................................................................50
    Duke Second Essay Prompt #2..................................................................54
    Personal or professional content?..............................................................62
    Think about it this way..............................................................................63
The Optional Essay..........................................................................................65
What to Do Next..............................................................................................66

# What to Know About Duke?

The million-dollar question is always, "Do I have a chance at....?" So let's kick off this *SnarkStrategies Guide* with an understanding of what Duke is about and who tends to be successful there.

Duke is in this interesting position: The brand name of the parent university is widely known and recognized throughout the world. Most would agree that Duke is a quality institution that attracts high-caliber students. Yet MBA snobs often say that Fuqua is not as good a school as Booth or Kellogg.

Yet we glance at the most recent BusinessWeek rankings (2012), and there it is at #6. It's held steady in that spot for a couple years now, which is most unusual. Unless your name is Stanford, Harvard, or Booth, most schools can expect to see their position in the BW list slip and slide from year to year. Duke almost could claim to be a Top 5 school! Almost.

By contrast, we see Duke way down at position #14 on the U.S. News ranking – which strikes us as a little unfair. Our take is that BusinessWeek has inflated Duke in relation to its peers, and U.S. News has cheated them. We aren't going to go into the minutiae of the different methodologies in use by these two publications, but suffice it to say, we've placed Duke at #7 – tied with Kellogg – on our own rankings list, which focuses on "ease of getting in" as the key metric for evaluation. You can see that list on the EssaySnark blahg here:

http://essaysnark.com/2014/05/a-ranking-of-the-best-mba-business-schools-just-like-businessweek-does/

Our take on school quality is based on the only data that we have direct knowledge of: The type of candidate who is accepted. We see the inputs and outputs of the MBA application process and we know the type of person that each school accepts. We know the people well, in fact – working with a Brave Supplicant on her application gives us tremendous insight into who she is and how she operates. Not only do we have the full history of test scores and transcripts and work experience, but we've interacted with her on rounds and rounds of essay revision and resume rework and often interview prep too.

This tells us about the person. And who the schools admit tells us about them.

We also collect data on the schools – the raw data of GMAT averages and 80% ranges and class sizes and acceptance rates. Looking at all of this data as an outsider, the opinion that we've formed is that Duke is a class act.

In our experience, it's harder to get into Duke than many other schools that you may assume to be its peer. And we heard Duke's Dean say in May that app volumes are increasing at Fuqua faster than they are at other schools. They got about 10% more applications last year than they had in the prior season. This is a very significant jump. Some schools even lost apps last year (MIT being one of them). Many schools saw volumes go up but we don't know of any other that increased in double-digits.

Duke is often lumped into a category along with Ross and Cornell and Darden. Those are fair assessments; they all have similar GMAT score averages and ranges, and their acceptance rates are actually all within the same band (25-30%). It is understandable for someone to assign Duke to that group of business school. Duke's numbers are certainly closer to those schools than to Wharton's or Chicago's. After all, Duke has a sub-700 average GMAT score. How good a school could it be?

However, watching the process unfold at Duke for many many years, we can tell you: It's much harder to get into Duke than it is Ross and the others. Having the same acceptance rate doesn't mean that their patterns of acceptance are the same.

This may be surprising to you. After all, the average GMAT score at Ross is currently over 700 – 704, to be exact, for the Class of 2015, the most recent figure available as of this writing (early July 2014). Shouldn't that indicate that it's harder to get in there?

You'd think that's the case. But it's not. Obviously EssaySnark is not working with the entire applicant pool – our numbers are limited, we don't have visibility into everyone applying at every school. However, we believe that Duke is more likely to choose a strong *person* over a strong *GMAT score.*

In fact, they seem to do things a little more like LBS does.

Hopefully everyone reading this will agree that London Business School is a top-notch program. Many people name LBS in the same sentence as Columbia and Wharton; yes, it's *that* good.

Yet the average GMAT score for LBS is much closer to Duke's than it is to Columbia's. Why this pattern? Why do LBS and Duke have lower average test scores even when they seem to be more selective in who they're accepting?

One reason is that they've both got decent-sized but not massive classes to fill. Duke and LBS both typically have from 400 to 440 students in each entering class. And they both get around 3,100 to 3,500 applications per year. While the makeup of their applicant pool is radically different – LBS gets far fewer Americans applying than Duke does, for obvious reasons – and the schools themselves offer totally unique educational experiences, the admissions committees in Durham and in London have an equivalent challenge of identifying the candidates who really understand what their respective schools are about and selecting those who will be a good fit to the culture and opportunity. This means going beyond the static measure of the GMAT score and looking at the entirety of the application, and also it means judging to see if the person has strong intent to accept an offer, should one be extended.

We've heard anecdotally that Fuqua, and LBS, often *reject* a good number of their highest-scoring applicants. We don't have data to back this up and it's solidly in the category of hearsay, but we have heard admissions folks at both these schools express dismay by the poor attitude they sometimes see in the essays that come in from candidates with very high test scores. If you're applying with a 750+, good on you! But your work has just begun; it's the essays and the entirety of your application that will matter most.

Another way that these two schools are alike is that they're both interested in older students. Both of them have multiple flavors of master's degrees, including a pre-experience Master's in Management. This lets them funnel off the well-qualified but younger candidates into a different educational track. They'll let you apply to the full-time MBA with no work experience, but they're not likely to admit you; only three students in the Class of 2014 came in straight from college.

This is to your advantage – if you've got more experience, then you probably want to be going to class with someone more at your level, or even more advanced, from whom you can learn. The older/wiser bschool student can contribute more to the classroom environment, and presumably they'll be better able to carry their weight on a team project. You don't want to be saddled with teaching your teammate the basics of entering an Excel equation or formatting a PPT when you're up against a deadline in compiling an important report in corporate finance.

We're not suggesting that if you're interested in Duke that you should also apply to LBS – though maybe you should. These two schools are different enough in terms of how their MBA programs are structured and the opportunities available after graduation that we would encourage you to research the offerings carefully before placing them both into your application strategy basket. We're not trying to paint the programs with the same brush. We're simply explaining some possible reasons behind the truth that we've observed at Duke: This is not a bschool that just anyone can waltz into. You'll need to have a strong application and put some time into developing your pitch.

If you have a high GMAT, then great, that's going to be a point in your favor. But it's not going to be enough to get you in. And if you have a lower score, then you maybe don't need to sweat it too much. Provided it's within a decent range – we'll discuss particulars in a minute – your GMAT score could very well be high enough to get you a green light from the Fuqua admissions team.

So, key takeaway messages from this first bit?

1. Your GMAT score is not the be-all/end-all bucks-stops-here factor in decision-making at Duke. A score below 700 — associated with a strong set of essays — has a real chance of success.

2. Younger students are not exactly encouraged for the Duke Daytime MBA, and in fact may be a better fit for the Master's in Management instead.

3. Older students, by contrast, are welcome at Duke Daytime, with experience levels often extending up to the 12+ years range.

4. The average age for the Duke Daytime MBA is 29 years, and a quarter of students are married, which are both higher numbers than you see at many schools.

Older applicants tend to have lower GMAT scores. Since Duke favors more experience, then that means they're willing to take the candidates who may have weakness in their test results but demonstrate that they'll add value in the program overall.

So when we say "it's harder to get into Duke" what we're talking about is the essays. You need to do a better job on your pitch to have a chance at this school.

Oh yeah, one more thing you should know about this school: It seems that they are not part of the collection of bschools that has standardized on recommender's questions. The Duke recommendation process will need to be completed on its own, using the specific Fuqua questions. Your recommenders will need to do this task separately from the identical two-question recommendations they will be submitting if you're applying to any of the subset of what we call "recommender-cooperative" schools including Harvard, Stanford, Columbia, Yale, and NYU (there may be others in this group as well). We're mentioning this now because you'll need to plan for this for your recommender strategy and prep, since it's different than they may encounter with writing recs for your other apps.

## What Is Duke Known For?

Now that you have a baseline understanding that Duke will be looking beyond just your core stats in evaluating your candidacy, lets look at what Duke is good at and why you might want to go there.

- Fuqua is known for its strength in the business of healthcare, as is its neighbor, UNC Kenan-Flagler. The RTP area is a hub for medicine, and there are many resources in the region for those interested in pharma and biotech as well. Duke has a Health Sector Management certificate available to students in any flavor of its MBA. Wharton and Kellogg are some other schools putting on a bigger push into healthcare however Duke was one of the earliest to focus on this area in business school and they have one of the larger programs.

- There's quite a bit of high tech in the Raleigh-Durham area, including a concentration of startups and even a smattering of video game companies. In fact, according to Forbes, high-tech employment is 14.7% of the Durham economy — fourth place behind Silicon Valley, Boston, and Boulder, Colorado. Those firms are not typically pro-MBA in their hiring practices, however there's a thriving venture community in the area. Duke has some business plan competitions that are open to students across the university. If you're interested in entrepreneurship, it's definitely not a bad place to be — and guess what? If you're interested in entrepreneurship in the health sector, this could be an AWESOME environment for you. The Dean has talked about synergies in this particular cross-section of industry. If you happen to be in a position to pursue that type of opportunity, you are likely to get a warm welcome from the Fuqua adcom.

- Often connected to the startup / entrepreneurship thing: Duke is one of the few business schools with a focus on product management. This isn't limited to software and technology but it's a key strength at this school. You can study brand management and marketing anywhere, but the formal discipline of product management is not always emphasized as it is here.

- If you want to explore a career in energy — either oil and gas, or sustainable energy — then Duke should be on your list. There's other schools strong in these areas too but Fuqua is a favorite among recruiters in these industries.

- We started off with the niches. We have yet to mention the core strength. Duke sends a lot of grads into consulting. They've got a well-established pipeline to companies like Accenture and Deloitte — and McKinsey, Bain and BCG too. About a quarter of each class goes into consulting. If that's what you want to do, then this is a good place to do it.

- Finance is also a viable path at Fuqua, though maybe not the easiest way to get to a bulge-bracket i-bank. If you're comfortable working at a good company like BofA, Citi or Wells Fargo, then Duke could be a fine choice for you. They send some grads to Goldman but not in huge numbers. There's definitely not a lot of PE and VC hiring out of Duke. Investment management is growing, however. If you're interested in finance, look carefully at what you want to do post-MBA before deciding on Duke (or any school, for that matter).

Hiring data matters but there's more to a school than the job you're going to get when you pop out the other end of it. What else can we tell you about Duke? Here's a random list – not 25 Things perhaps, but a few worth mentioning:

- Duke has the amazing Professor Dan Ariely on faculty. He studies behavioral economics and he's a bit of a superstar. If you are not familiar with Dan, just go here: http://youtu.be/ZGGxguJsirl

- If you want to go to a great business school but you're either a) not certain that your profile is quite up to the challenge, and/or b) concerned about the costs and leaning towards a part-time program, then you might consider the Duke Cross-Continent MBA. This has been around for about five years now and it was designed as a hybrid, with an online or virtual classroom experience integrated with on-site sessions for two weeks every semester. The on-sites are residencies held in cities around the world, making it truly a global experience. The Cross-Continent admissions team is always up for discussing your profile with you – yes, before you apply – to see if it might be a good fit.

- Duke has a pre-experience Master's in Management for those wanting to go to bschool early on in their careers. They call it the Foundations of Business and it is essentially the core curriculum that you'd get in the first year of any MBA program. There's also a Master's in Engineering Management with both an on-campus and a distance-learning option. The one caution we'd offer if you're considering these programs is that you may be limiting your earnings potential more than you realize. Your first post-Master's job determines your lifetime earnings potential and those coming out with these MiM degrees typically have a much lower starting salary than with the MBA. Check out some posts on the EssaySnark blahg about this if you're unclear. You may want to go get a job for a few years and then come at the MBA application with some work experience under your belt, and you'd be in a stronger position in the end.

Before we talk about some details of the Duke application and how they manage their admissions processes, we should call out the key attribute of the Duke experience and what they're about. Many schools have a defining characteristic and this is true at Fuqua as well. For example, Harvard is known for *leadership*. That's certainly an important quality at Duke too but it's not the hallmark feature. Instead, Duke is known for –

Wait. We shouldn't have to tell you this. You should know this already.

If you can't fill in the *"Duke is about _____"* sentence, then you probably need to be doing more research on your own first. This MBA application guide won't do you much good if you haven't hit the pavement – virtual or otherwise – and learned what this school is about through your own efforts already. Putting in that effort is probably more important at Duke than it is at Harvard even. This is because of the values in place at this school.

## What you won't get here

That last paragraph should have given you a hint, but we're going to be explicit about this, particularly since Duke has introduced this Option 2 prompt for the second essay, which asks you to talk about their culture through the Fuqua Principles.

Fuqua has a couple of buzzwords or themes that are part of their culture, and are referenced on their website in various places, and this year, even more directly in their essay questions. These concepts are core to the Fuqua culture. We strongly recommend that you do your research on Duke, so that you are familiar with all such elements. (If you already have done that research, you probably know what we're talking about already.)

We don't like spoonfeeding people with the information that they should be getting on their own. Sorry if that seems unfair. As we've said before, we already got into bschool – we earned it. You need to do some of that 'earning' too – you can't just plunk down a couple bucks and expect the secrets of the universe to be handed over.

If you've read the other *SnarkStrategies Guides* then you already know that we won't tell you what a school like this is about. You need to find that out for yourself. More directly, we will not explain or expand upon these Principles that the adcom has defined for you. We won't do your thinking for you; you need to apply your own thought process to the essays.

We'll tell you a story – this one is about Haas but it totally applies here, too, since Berkeley's Defining Principles are so similar in certain ways to what Duke is doing with its Fuqua Principles thing.

We had a client several years ago who, as we started working together on his Berkeley app, was completely misunderstanding their Defining Principles. Now, to be fair, it's easy to misunderstand them; they're a little obtuse. It often takes some wrassling to get your head around what they're about. That's true with one or two of Fuqua's, too, so be prepared for some mental effort and digging to get a grasp on their true meaning.

Anyway, this Haas client wanted to use a particular accomplishment from his professional life in his main essay. That made sense to us, and it was a fine accomplishment to be presenting to any bschool; he was a high-powered consultant with some high-powered story of saving an important project from a prolonged and belabored death. But, he was convinced that he was talking about one of the Haas Defining Principles through his use of this story, and he just wasn't.

We went back and forth on it for weeks. Each time, we told him that we did not think his story fit the Defining Principle as we understood it. He was very stubborn and was insisting on doing it his way. At a certain point EssaySnark gave in. "Fine," we said. "These are your essays. You should absolutely go with what you feel is the right direction."

Hint: If you ever get that sort of feedback from us, that means you are being an idiot and we are giving up on you.

Then he attended an information session at Berkeley (thankfully at least he listened to our advice to go do that!. At the presentation, he heard some students or the admissions people or whomever talking about their Defining Principles. And he realized he was waaaaay off with how he'd been interpreting them.

**It is not our job to think for you.** If we work with you one-on-one as a client, we will respond to what you write and tell you if we think you've nailed it (or not). But we will never spell out to a client what they should say in an essay nor even how they should interpret the question. So we won't be doing that here for you and Duke either. It's up to you to interpret and reflect on the Fuqua questions, and on their own six Principles, and see where you take your awareness of that and integrate it into your essays based on the insights you gather and the conclusions you come to. You need to figure out for yourself where Duke is coming from on these. Having us regurgitate our own interpretation is not going to add value to your process. You need to discover it for yourself. That way, when you talk about it, your understanding will shine through and that will resonate with your audience.

So that's where we stand on that. There's still plenty of valuable information for you here.

Like this next section.

## What's Important at Duke

The Duke adcom wants to get to know you through the application process. That's why they've designed their questions this way; it's a true opportunity for you as the candidate to share some of who you are. Canned answers and essays that are obviously written to impress the reader rather than to communicate something real (particularly Essay 2) are not the way to go.

That's one reason why we won't be telling you what to say in any essay. We will offer advice on how not to do it – again, essay 2 in particular seems to trip people up when they're not paying attention. But there's not much more we can say except "be yourself." That's the only way you're going to deliver a list of 25 Things that's interesting and not nausea-inducing.

As with many schools, a critical part of the entire application will be your responses to the short-answer questions about career goal We'll be discussing that at length.

For Essay 2, regardless of which option you choose, the most critical angle for you to impart is, Do you know what this school is about?

What outreach have you done?

What can you say about your reasons for wanting to go there?

What would you tell *your best friends* when you're talking to them about it?

The Duke adcom is well aware of the fact that many BSers use them as a safety school. They need to be convinced that you are choosing them for their own values and strengths. They are not inclined to admit candidates unless they believe you'll say yes to them. They don't overcommit and invite everyone; they only accept candidates who are strong, and who are committed to their school.

You can apply to Duke as a second-choice school and still make it in, but you'd better be prepared to do the work and make the application shine with your convictions if you want that to happen.

By highlighting the activities you've been involved with in your life and the interests you have through the 25 Things essay, you'll be able to communicate that you share the values that Duke stands for.

By being clear and succinct with your short-answer responses, you'll be able to tell them why you want an MBA.

And by being honest and authentic in your answers for Essay 2, you'll be able to convince them why they should let you get that MBA at Duke.

In fact, this can be encapsulated as

## Snarky Strategy #1

> The Duke short-answer questions explain why you need an MBA.
> Essay 2 explains why you want to go to Duke to get it.
> Essay 1 shows how you are the type of person who *should* go to Duke.

Bschools want accomplished students. They want well-rounded students. They want students who will be engaged in their communities and do something with the opportunity. The Duke essays let you communicate how you are all that.

# The Interview and Your Duke Application Strategy

When you're applying to Duke, you should take into account your interview strategy, right upfront. Duke wants you to come to campus for your interview. The best time to do that is before you've submitted your application. Here's the ideal sequence of events:

1. Figure out career goals
2. Get essays to at least draft 2 or 3
3. Prep for interview
4. Visit campus and have your interview
5. Revise the essays with new info from campus visit

That exact sequence can be tough to pull off for Duke Early Action, given that the first open interview is in right before the deadline. So there's some logistical questions for you to juggle as you figure out when is the right time to make your trip to Raleigh-Durham. But if you can pull it off, such that you interview BEFORE you finalize and submit your essays, you will be setting yourself up for the best of all possible worlds.

If you're applying to Duke through any other round, then they're giving you this major advantage. The best opportunity of all for doing a great job with your applications is the applicant-initiated interview, conducted before you submit. And you can do that with Duke's Open Interview.

## *Open Interview*

Duke offers an Open Interview from September through mid-October. This means that you can request the interview – you don't have to wait for the adcom to invite you. The Open Interview period is a very limited-time window within which you can travel to Durham, do a campus tour, sit in on a class, and, of course, have your admissions interview. The interview is typically with a specially-trained second-year student. The interview is an important part of any successful application to business school and in this case, getting to request the interview yourself is a key strategy that you should take advantage of.

Yes, you should do this even if you're not based in the U.S.

If you are based in the U.S. - even if you're on the West Coast, which means you're technically exempt from doing it – and even if you're not applying in the Early Action round – you should *definitely* do the Open Interview process.

If you're reading this after mid-October and the opportunity is past, don't worry, it's not the end of the world. It doesn't mean your chances are screwed. If the Duke adcom decides that they want to meet you, they'll issue an invite and you'll be able to interview with them when they travel to a city near you. There's a list of 20 or so different locations where they will be having interviews in this admissions season. Doing an adcom-initiated interview is no disadvantage.

But doing the applicant-initiated interview can be one.

Our experience is that those who get on campus and go for the interview when it's offered *have better Essay 2 essays than those who do not*.

Beyond that very important fact, going to campus ahead of time also shows tremendous initiative and motivation. After all, you are going out of your way, at inconvenience and expense, to travel to campus and do the interview *even though it's not required*.

This also shows that you have your act together and planning ahead. You're being thorough. You wouldn't have even known about the Open Interview period in order to take advantage of the opportunity if you had not been doing your research early.

This interview policy is different from many schools and you need to do some learning about Duke in order to even realize that it's a possibility. And you need to be doing all this well in advance of their first deadlines in order to take advantage of it.

All of that bodes well for you as an applicant. It shows that you're prepared and doing this the right way.

The person for whom the Open Interview is *especially* recommended is the reapplicant. If you tried for Duke last year and didn't make it in, then you should DEFINITELY head to North Carolina and do the interview experience this time – yes, even if you did it before. You should do this whether you're applying in Early Action or Round 1 deadlines.

In fact, this one is so important that we're going to codify it as such.

# Snarky Strategy #2

## Take advantage of Duke's Open Interview period. Do the on-campus interview even if you're an international applicant. Do it especially if you're a reapplicant. And do it regardless of which round you're planning on applying in.

Some people assume, because of the timing, that this Open Interview option is only for the Early Action round, and that's just not true. You can plan to apply in ANY round and go through the Open Interview process. It can be beneficial to you, in terms of learning about what the school is about and how the culture is different, and you can weave those learnings into your essays. It can add tremendous value to your application and give you a real leg up.

No, they won't admit someone with a lousy set of essays just because they did one of these on-campus interviews. But it sure can help.

Here's another way it can help:

## Your application fee will be reduced if you do it.

Duke has this generous policy of finding ways to lower – or even eliminate – the fee you will pay for applying. If you're a Peace Corps or Teach for America alumna/us, or if you're active duty U.S. military or honorably discharged within the past three years, then there's no application fee to apply to Duke. However, even if you're just a plain old Joe (or Jose, or Jay, or Jaya) then you still have this great opportunity to get a reduced fee: You can visit campus and they'll cut the application charge to just $125. You can get this reduction even if you attend an official Duke information session in your part of the world – you don't technically have to fly to North Carolina to qualify. Yet as you can see, EssaySnark thinks that you should put forth the effort.

## Everyone should interview on campus

Nobody is a shoo-in at any top school. Even though Duke has a higher acceptance rate than many other schools, they still get a lot of applications. There's tremendous competition for the 400 or so seats in the next entering class. If you want to make sure that you have the best chance possible for landing one of those, then we'd encourage you to pull out the stops.

But honestly, that's not the reason to go interview on campus. The adcom has implemented that reduced application fee policy as a very obvious incentive: **they want you to learn about who they are**. If you can't make it to Durham for the Open Interview period – because you found out too late or for whatever other reason – then plan on going to campus if (when!) they invite you to interview.

# Snarky Strategy #3

## Plan to *go to Duke* for your interview – regardless of when that interview happens.

Duke is one of the few schools that actively encourages these campus visits – obviously they do, or they wouldn't have this whole Open Interview period in the first place. They prefer that anyone who's invited for the interview does so on the Duke University campus. This is not mandatory, but they actively encourage it. When you complete your application, you'll have a chance to indicate where you'd want to interview, should they invite you for one. EssaySnark suggests that you go along with the admissions team's recommendation and mark down Durham for your interview.

Obviously you should not do that if you know that you would never follow through. It would be seriously lame to have to tell them you can't, once they issue that invite later on. That won't look so good. It wouldn't be the end of the world but it wouldn't be a positive, either. Only do this if you actually will make it happen when the time comes to go through the interview experience. It will be worth it all the way around.

Basically what we're saying is, if you want to go to Duke, it wouldn't hurt to *go to Duke*. An applicant to any of the Top 20 bschools in the world would benefit from visiting and understanding what the school is about. With Duke, it's more than that. The adcom is signaling every way that they can that they want you to visit during the application process. If you have massive weaknesses in your profile (especially if there's more than one) or if you're applying from an oversubscribed candidate pool like Indians in IT or white guys in finance, then it would be smart for you to visit.

We don't have hard numbers that show that applicants who visit are more likely to get admitted – but we'd be willing to bet that they are. It's not a causal relationship; the school won't be accepting you *because* you visited. Instead, it's correlated: the person who visits tends to have more going for themselves, and they're better able to make the most of the opportunity by leveraging what they learn in the essays, and making a better pitch all around.

Preparing for your interview will require some dedicated time and effort. We've got another *SnarkStrategies* for that, which you may want to pick up after you've gotten your Duke essays together. The Duke interviews are all blind – the interviewer will only have your resume, they will not have read anything else about you, and they won't have access to your essays if you're on an adcom-initiated interview after submitting your app. The best time to do your interview prep is within two weeks before the interview. If you're doing the Open Interview, then we're guessing that this may be the first interview you've done for awhile, unless you've recently gone through the experience for a new job. If that's the case, then prep and practice will be even more important. Don't skip this part of the process – you don't want to just show up on campus and think you can wing it. Interviews are not often a make-or-break situation but they definitely are factored into the admissions decisions. Take it seriously. Go in prepared and you'll walk out feeling confident.

To make this decision-making easy on you, and for those who like to see pretty charts and graphs, here's the simple version:

| | |
|---|---|
| **Best Option** | On-Campus Open Interview<br><br>This is **highly recommended** regardless of which round you're applying in; it's mandatory if you're applying Early Action from most of the U.S. |
| **Next-Best Option** | Select "Durham" in the interview request section on application.<br><br>Then, plan to travel to Duke if (when!) they invite you to interview. |
| **Last-Best Option** | Select any other location in the interview request section.<br><br>You might interview with an alumni or, if the admissions team is traveling to your part of the world, you will interview with a member of the adcom. |
| **To-Be-Avoided Option** | If you have no possible way around it, you can request for alternate interview arrangements.<br><br>You should only do this if you have a really good reason (see below). |

Regardless of who you interview with (student, alumni, admissions committee member) the interviews are all weighed the same. The actual interview experience will be quite different; we go into that in the EssaySnark Interviewing Guide. But any interview counts equally with all the rest.

If you're deployed with the military or on assignment with the Peace Corps or something, then they'll arrange a Skype interview. However, unless you have such extenuating circumstances (like, you're in Afghanistan and there's just not that many Fuqua alum hanging around in the hills and available to interview you) then you should not request for special arrangements like that.

An interview is required for admission.

## Duke and Early Action

You're probably aware that Duke has the traditional three admissions rounds, plus Early Action.

If you're in love with Duke already and you really really want to go there, apply Early Action.

If not, apply Round 1.

Yes, Early Action is an advantage over Round 1 – but it's not something that you can mess around with. You're allowed to apply to other schools (except for Columbia) while you have a Duke EA application pending, but as soon as they admit you, that means that you'll pull your apps from any other schools and you'll pay your deposit to Duke. It means you're going to Duke. It's non-negotiable.

They put some very specific language into their online application around the Early Action round, which you agree to abide by if you submit in that option.

Early Action is a promise: You promise to go there if they agree to let you in.

It's not an insurance policy to use in case your app to some other school doesn't work out.

Recently, Duke even included some specific language in the Early Action agreement that says you authorize them to contact other schools to inform them that you have been accepted through Early Action. The schools do talk to each other. The other schools respect these policies. If one admissions board hears that you've been accepted through Early Action at Duke – and they know that you haven't withdrawn your application from consideration for their program – do you think they're going to be inclined to admit you? You would be showing poor judgment indeed.

Why risk it? If Duke isn't 100% your first-choice school, then there's no need to bother with this sneakiness and potential deception. Just apply in their Round 1 and you're fine.

It's not like everyone who applies in Early Action is admitted. You're not increasing your chances *that* much. If you're uncomfortable with the commitment upfront, then just don't make it. Don't put yourself in that position. Easy decision.

The major advantage with Duke Early Action is that *it's really early*. They issue decisions for this program super fast. Once you go through that cycle – if you're denied – then every other school's application processing will seem to take ages. Especially if you apply to Haas or MIT; they tend to take the longest to issue decisions. But not Duke EA. They're the fastest of all, faster even than Columbia's goal of eight weeks to decision. It's pretty impressive, actually.

And that can be a very big advantage. If you try for Duke EA and you don't get in, then you have plenty of time to regroup and rework your strategy for another school. You could even hit a school like Tuck's November Round or NYU Round 2.

And if you apply to Duke and you get in? You'll be celebrating when everyone else is still worried about when the interview invites are going to start coming.

One reason that they can move through the process so quickly for the EA applicants is because of that Open Interview period. Anyone from most parts of the U.S. would've already gone through the interview by the time that the applications are due. So that's one logistical issue taken care of. And there just aren't huge quantities of candidates who are applying from other parts of the world who will put Duke as their #1 choice. (Tip: That means it's easier for you to stand out in the EA round, if you're applying from overseas. Again, provided that they are your first choice and you'd be happy to go there for your MBA.)

It's totally fine to be submitting other applications while your Duke EA app is in play – the only exception being Columbia. You can't simultaneously apply to both Columbia in their Early Decision option, and to Duke. You must pick one or the other, since both are binding. You can, however, apply to Tuck's Early Action option, which is not binding. Those are the main schools that have these "early" options today. Any other school is fair game to try for while the Duke Early Action application is being processed – but remember, even if Harvard has just invited you to interview, you have to say "no" and withdraw your application the moment that Duke says "yes."

Think it through.

Oh yeah, one last thing about Duke and Early Action: Despite the rumors to the contrary, they do award scholarship money to people that they accept in this round.

There's some language on the Duke website that says something about how, if scholarship awards are very important to you, that the Early Action round may not be the right one for you. Many people interpreted that to mean that they are forcing those accepted through EA to go to Duke with no financial assistance, even though the applicant would otherwise qualify for it. This is bogus baloney.

All that language is there for is because of some lame-o applicants who applied in Early Action – and didn't pull their apps from other schools, which then awarded them some money with their admits. And then they went to Duke with their hand out, asking for Duke to match the offer. And Duke said no – not because they don't award any money in EA, but because they weren't going to award it *to them*. And why would they, at that point? The applicant was clearly violating the EA policy by not withdrawing the other applications.

When you're applying to business school, you need to go into it under the assumption that you're not going to get awarded ANY money. You are just trying to get IN. This situation is so competitive, with so many variables and unknowns and different possible outcomes, that you should be maximizing your chances of acceptance – that is all.

The only way you can go into it trying for some scholarship money as part of your admit is if you a) have a VERY high GMAT score and you b) are applying to VERY low-ranked schools. If you come into a school like Emory or Vanderbilt and you have a GMAT in the 760 range, then yes, it's possible that they may find some scholarship money to help you make your decision. A high GMAT score helps their rankings significantly. It would be a big gain to have you on board.

If you're an underrepresented U.S. minority (Black, Hispanic, Native American) then there's a good chance you might get some offers of funding, too. This is just because of how the schools are all motivated to increase diversity among the student body.

If you're like most of the Brave Supplicants that we work with … no. You're not likely to get a lot of help with your graduate business education. Don't expect it. Just do the best job you can on the applications and hope that you get the offer. Most people don't have that much trouble coming up with the funding required (from student loans) once they're admitted.

Duke has a no-cosigner loan available for international applicants.

And Duke definitely DOES award scholarship money to Early Action admittees.

Here's direct from Duke Admissions when we asked them about this:

> Thank you, EssaySnark & Team, for reaching out to us about the Early Action and Scholarship misconception – because it is one!
>
> We, too, have heard the rumors fly and addressed the questions last year through a blog post from our Director of Admissions, Megan Lynam. http://blogs.fuqua.duke.edu/duke-mba/admissions/2012/08/31/is-early-action-right-for-me/ referencing item 4, in particular.

We also did a full post on the EssaySnark blahg about this, in case you want more details – you can see it here: http://essaysnark.com/2013/07/duke-early-action-and-scholarship-money/

In fact, here's the entirety of the email we got from the successful Brave Supplicant quoted on the front cover:

```
Hi Snark,

Just wanted to let you know - I got admitted to
Fuqua and I'll be matriculating the next fall! As
opposed to the "common knowledge" regarding early
rounds (you also wrote about it in the blahg), I
even got a flattering scholarship.

Your feedback (through the "Rejection Analysis" was
definitely worth the money and proved to be highly
valuable in drafting my applications afterwards. I
have incorporated many of your comments and
suggestions (mostly regarding my career goals,
resume and work experience) into my Duke
applications, and I guess that it really showed
through.
```

This person had gone it alone the prior season and it didn't work out. We fully dissected that unsuccessful app through our Post-Mortem process, and apparently that was a valuable step to take! We're offering this up to emphasize the value of Early Action, and to show you that reapplicants do get in, and to also offer proof that an Early Action candidate still qualifies for scholarship awards.

Duke Early Action is all advantage and no downside–provided, again, that Duke is your first choice.

## Duke and other rounds

If you're not comfortable with signing away all your bschool options in advance and you don't want to do Early Action, no problem. Like other top schools, Duke Round 1 is also a great choice, and for most people, it's probably the better way to go.

And if you're coming at this a little later in the season, all is not lost. Duke Round 2 in January is also a feasible strategy. If you're still working on getting your GMAT score up, then it's likely going to be a better plan to push your application out till later in the season and apply with a stronger GMAT score. That's almost always the case; even though Duke can be flexible on the GMAT score for a candidate they otherwise like, you don't want them to have to make compromises when they're reviewing your application. It's always better if you give them reason to believe in you all across the board. A higher GMAT score in a later round is often the right tradeoff to make.

The only rule in the round strategy game is, Round 3 at Duke should be avoided. This is true regardless of what part of the world you're coming from, but it's particularly true if you're an international candidate. The other disadvantage with Round 3 is that most of the scholarship money has been awarded, and you also will have missed the Duke Admit Weekends. So it's not ideal all around – and it's also got a much lower chance of success.

If you're thinking about Round 3, our advice is to wait it out till the next admissions season, which – believe us – will be here before you know it.

If you're bound and determined to try in Round 3, then make sure you have a strong application – stronger than what we've been saying could work in an earlier round. Your GMAT score and your GPA need to be HIGHER if you're trying in the final round, and there needs to be something compelling about your profile, in terms of uniqueness or originality. If you're just another Indian engineer with a 710 GMAT, it's going to be near impossible. You cannot expect to skate by with a less-competitive application in the most-competitive round.

## Duke and Debt

Before we move on to the essays, we have to mention one unfortunate fact about Duke, which is that Duke has hit the #1 spot among all business schools in a not-great category: Student debt load upon graduation. That causes a very big frowny face from EssaySnark. This ignoble #1 spot has also been taking by Wharton and Tuck in recent years (and depending on who you're asking to do the calculations) but Duke is often in the top three. We heard Duke's Dean mention this in Spring 2014 so it's definitely something they're quite aware of in Durham.

We're not certain of the reasons for this (he didn't elaborate) and we found this to be surprising. It's actually much less expensive to live in North Carolina than it is at many other cities where top bschools are located. The first-year program costs for Duke are comparable to other out-of-the-way schools like Cornell - $82,006 at Fuqua, compared to $81,892 at Johnson – and these figures are way lower than many schools' (Stanford is $99,435; yes, Stanford will cost you about $35,000 more for your MBA than Duke will).

This high debt statistic could be due to Duke's rather large number of international students, who often need to take out more loans, and those loans are expensive. Yes, Duke has a no-cosigner-required lender available for international students to use, however the rates for these loans are higher than domestic loans, coming in around 8.25% for the past few years (it's Prime Rate +3%).

Another factor could be because of their liberal policy on accepting non-traditional applicants who tend to make less money pre-MBA and so will be more active borrowers than someone who comes into bschool from finance or consulting. Both of those factors could easily play into that sad statistic, and both of those factors are actually positives when you consider them in the grand scheme of things. Another theory is that because Duke goes for older applicants, then it may be less likely that they have parents footing the bill than you'd get with a younger bschool student population.

A small contributor to this could also be that Duke doesn't have an emergency loan fund where students can apply for short-term cash distributions to cover unexpected situations. Other schools do have this, which can be a lifesaver. The lack of this offering surely is not responsible for putting Duke at the top of this unhappy list but it can't help.

Our best bet for why Duke ranks high? It could be because they are more generous in allowing students to add optional items to their Cost of Attendance budget, which determines how much debt they can take on. Every school publishes an estimated Cost of Attendance for the coming academic year. Some schools intentionally inflate this number to give students more leeway in how much they can individually borrow. For example, a common line item on many schools' Cost of Attendance calculation is a laptop. But who doesn't have a laptop these days? It used to be that students had to buy a laptop – sometimes even a certain recommended brand or configuration – as part of their on-boarding process. Many schools still include this expense in their COA estimate, typically around $2,500, which is in your favor even if you don't need to buy one for class. It gives you more flexibility in how much you choose to borrow. For Duke, the laptop expense is not included in the base COA, but it can be added on to your individual estimate. There seem to be more categories of these add-on expenses that Fuqua students can take advantage of than some other schools offer. If you have the chance to bump up your allowable borrowing amount, then many people will do just that, since you're typically pretty strapped for cash as you go through bschool. There's no paycheck coming in every few weeks, and that is a real shock to the system (we talk about these considerations in *The Accepted Student's Guide* and how to financially prepare for your MBA, which you may want to look for once you're admitted).

Maxing out your borrowing options is rather common for bschool students, and a very cursory review of the choices that Duke provides indicates to us that they may be allowing for more of these add-ons than some other schools. This obviously means that you then end up with Duke grads having comparatively bigger loan balances on graduation.

We wish that Duke would do some analysis and share this with the public; we haven't seen any of that before and it would be nice to get some context and greater understanding around the causal factors, instead of leaving us to guessing.

Please remember that having a higher debt load says nothing about your future earnings potential. Duke is in line with its peers with average exit salaries. There's no need to worry about your ability to pay off your loans.

We take this datapoint in the same context as we do Duke's lower average GMAT score: They're looking for PEOPLE to admit to their program – not numbers. And they're very open-minded on who they will accept.

## Your Duke Strategy

With your Duke application, you need to do what you need to do with many bschool apps: You need to explain why you want an MBA, in the context of what you want to do with the degree when you graduate. Those career goals need to be sharply defined and clearly expressed. There is no room for extraneous words in your short-answer responses. You'll need to cut to the chase and actually tell them what you plan to do. These questions are some of the hardest you'll encounter at any school – not because they are overly complicated, but because they require you to be so concise. In our experience, that's not what most BSers are good at.

Where do you explain yourself? How do you make the goals more real? You get a perfect opportunity to do that in Essay 2.

Among all three of these deliverables to Duke, you need to have enough details to show how the goals are real for you, that you've put some thought into them and you're in a position to make such a jump or transition based on your background and the experiences you bring to the table.

You also need to come across as a real person. This is where Essay 1 comes in, but it's also key (very key) for Essay 2.

Sometimes we see essays written for bschool apps that appear to have come from a robot. People sound like automatons in their writing, or they trot out the million-dollar words in an attempt to sound smart. Keep your thesaurus in its dusty spot on the bookshelf. Don't be tempted to use lofty writing and fancy phrases. Write in a simple way that authentically sounds like you – with clear examples and good stories – and you're more than halfway there to an admit at Duke.

The other key ingredient for a Duke application is to present compelling evidence that you'll choose them. The adcom is very protective of their school. They seek to only accept candidates who are serious about them. Writing essays that convey this is definitely more art than science, but mostly where it comes through is when the applicant *really feels that way*.

The adcoms have this weird sixth sense where they can pick up on it if you're faking.

In fact there's not a whole lot more we can say about it except that if you're applying to Duke as a safety school, then make sure you still do the requisite legwork in knowing why it's a good place for you to get an MBA. Don't cut corners in how you present that to the adcom – a safety school app still needs the same amount of work and revision as a first-choice school. Especially in this case, where they will be scrutinizing your pitch.

In the online application, almost every school asks you to tell them what other schools you're applying to. You could choose not to answer this (though we don't recommend that) or you could massage your list to disclose only the ones you think are the "correct answer" to that question. But you should recognize that the schools can see which other schools your GMAT score reports have been sent to, so lying in that answer is sort of senseless.

If you are applying to a list like Kellogg, Columbia, Tuck ... and Duke ... well, Duke may assume that they're playing second fiddle in that group. Your ability to convince them otherwise becomes that much more important.

The irony of course is that often people start out by thinking that Duke is not among their first-choice programs... but then they begrudgingly do this work in terms of research and outreach to the Duke community... maybe they even get on a plane and visit. And what frequently happens is, Duke slowly inches its way up the BSer's list of schools until it's at or near the top.

Duke knows that this can happen. They have confidence in the strength of their culture. This is the main reason that they put such emphasis on it when they are encouraging you to visit. If you do, they know that the chances are good you'll decide they're your favorite.

Kinda cool and sneaky all at the same time.

So, for many reasons, you need to pound the pavement – or make good use of your inbox and your phone. Connect with people at Duke. Take notes on why you like them. Identify their strengths and figure out what makes them a good fit for you. And be prepared to articulate that in Essay 2, and in conversations with your second-year student ambassador in your interview when the opportunity arises.

This idea of "school fit" matters A LOT at Duke, and you need to pull out all the stops in convincing the adcom that you're in love with them. You need details here. You'll need to express an understanding of what Fuqua can offer, based on how you talk about the opportunities you'd be afforded by going there.

If you want to go to Duke, you'll need to make it a priority to do significant research and learn about who they are and what they offer. Plan to devote some time to this.

## One more comment on the Duke application

There's more than one question on the Duke application that sends Brave Supplicants into tizzy fits. The other one we're talking about is the question about "have you worked with an agency or consultant on your application?" EssaySnark's advice? Just tell the truth.

Reading this *SnarkStrategies Guide* is not "working with a consultant" – you can honestly answer "no" even though you're using this book. If you've had actual help on your applications, in any form or format, from us or any other consultants out there, then the answer is "yes" and it seems to us you should just go ahead and say so.

Remember, they have that Honor Code thing. Sure, you can lie… but why would you? There's no shame in getting help on your applications. When you're doing your taxes, or dealing with a legal question, or have a medical issue, you seek out advice of a professional. Applying to bschool is the same thing. Seeking help from a professional who is familiar with the landscape is no big deal. Fuqua is cool with it. They know that there are ethical consultants out there.

They even talk to some of them, sometimes. Or so we've heard. ☺

There's one other warning that we want to alert you about regarding the Duke MBA application: If you get in, you'll need to pay a deposit – of course. That's required at all schools. The Early Action round requires a non-refundable $3,000 around the first of December – yes, before most other Round 1 schools release decisions. They schedule that for a reason. The other rounds require a $2,000 deposit at later dates in the season, though the deposit deadline for Round 1 is also earlier than you can expect to get final decisions from your Round 2 schools. You can check the due dates on Duke's website. Unless you applied in Early Action, you can of course pay your deposit and then change your mind if another school that you'd prefer to go to accepts you afterward, but don't expect to get any money back from Duke if you do. You can do that with Early Action too but then you're just a schmuck.

What's not as widely known is this: They don't accept credit cards for the deposit payment. You'll need to send in a check (or maybe they do wire transfer; EssaySnark is not sure). You will of course get all the details on this policy when you're admitted, but we wanted to make you aware of it now. Not everyone has a couple grand laying around in their bank accounts, ready to be sent off in a check – a check! Who writes checks anymore?! We're not sure of the reason behind the policy, but figured you might want to know.

We're getting a little ahead of ourselves though. Doesn't matter about paying a deposit fee, what matters is getting your ducks in a row so that you have a chance to get admitted in the first place.

## Duke Evaluation Criteria

Lots of schools say that they review applications holistically, but then you look at their statistics and you see that most people who get in have a high GMAT and an impressive GPA. While Duke definitely cares about GMAT and GPA, they're not as fixated on the numbers as some other adcoms seem to be.

### *GMAT*

The average GMAT score at Duke is a tick below 700 – which is 20 points lower than the top-ranked schools. This reflects the fact that Duke is competing with a broader spectrum of business schools for their candidates. It also shows that they value other things beyond the GMAT. Just because you have a high test score doesn't mean you can waltz into a place like this. They need to see what you bring to the table beyond the ability to do well on standardized tests.

If your GMAT is in the upper 600s or better, then you're fine on that count. The 80% range for Duke has been stable for many years at around 640 to 740, which is both a broader range, and anchored lower on the spectrum, than we see at other schools. We discussed before that Duke is looking at the whole person. Don't be dissuaded if your GMAT score is a little lower – but also, don't assume it's "good enough" if you know you can do better. A higher GMAT is always preferred, by any admissions person, as it shows you put in the studying required and that you'll do well in their school.

## A Snarky Caveat

### Duke is one of the few schools that expressly prefers the GMAT.

They'll accept a GRE score, because everyone does now and they'd be lame to not do so. But they don't want to. Duke states specifically on their website that they would rather see a GMAT score as part of your application (go to Daytime MBA → Admissions and choose Selection Criteria in the table in the middle of the page, then expand the Academic Aptitude and Quantitative Proficiency section; yeah, we find their website difficult to navigate, too).

If all you've got is a GRE, then apply with the GRE. But if you have a choice in the matter, go with the GMAT.

## Grades

Just like with the GMAT, a better academic record puts you in a stronger position when it comes to getting in. The average GPA at Duke is currently around 3.4, which is lower than many schools. They still require a level of academic competence. If your GPA is below 3.0 on the 4.0 scale, be prepared to take action before applying – the EssaySnark blahg has plenty of advice on what to do about a low GPA. If your worst grades were in quantitatively difficult classes, and you also did poorly on the quant side of the GMAT, then you definitely need to take care of that double-whammy weakness before you apply. If the rest of your story is sound then you may turn out fine.

## A Snarky Caveat

> Don't assume anything just because the averages are lower at Duke. You still need to put in the effort and give them a reason to accept you.

Which, of course, you're willing to do. You're reading this book, aren't you?

## Older Applicant

Another area where we see Duke be more flexible at times is with the older candidate – including even some Indians who are past 30 (gasp!). That cohort tends to be trickier than most in its ability to land a spot at a top MBA program. Certain schools are more open to thirty-somethings and Duke is among them.

Duke does prefers *some* work experience – you're going to have a tough time getting in if you're trying straight out of college. At least two years is a good starting point. But they tend to prefer significant experience – at least five years is smart, and even more can be just fine. Even with 10+ years in the workforce, it's still possible to make a compelling case for the Daytime MBA that the Duke adcom will accept.

## Reapplying to Duke

If you tried to get into Duke last year and didn't make it, then we encourage you to include them on your list again. Duke is more welcoming to reapplicants than almost any other program. They will want you to show how you've improved your profile, but they'll give you a fair shake and will be very open-minded when they evaluate your app this time. The reason? Because you're showing commitment. It means that, regardless of how you felt about them last time, this year you're more likely to put them in a higher position on your list – they still may not be your first choice but it's doubtful that you're trying to use them as a safety school now.

The other reason that Duke likes reapplicants is because *they're humble*. Not getting into bschool is one of the most demoralizing things that can happen to a young person. If you were at all cocky in your assumptions about getting in the first time, then now you won't be. You'll be hungry. You'll want it more. And you're probably going to do a better job now, due to an enhanced appreciation and respect for the challenges. All of that can be appealing to the adcom; and yes, it comes through on the page.

We have one tip for a reapplicant – this loosely applies for any school where you may be riding the merry-go-round a second time:

### Snarky Strategy #4

> Reapplicants should apply in Early Action.
> Or Round 1 at the latest. Don't wait for Round 2.
> And you should do your darnedest to do the
> Open Interview

These strategies are *strongly recommended* – in fact, the Duke adcom recommends it.

Let's tackle the first piece:

To submit a reapp in Duke Early Action communicates loud and clear where you're coming from.

If you just can't do that – if you have your irons in the fire at other schools and you're honestly not sure which one you'd want to say "yes" to, should you have the privilege of multiple offers, then no. Don't do EA. Wait to Round 1. It's fine to do so.

But it's certainly preferred to do Early Action. Again, only if you're good with the commitment!

The most important advice is don't lose your edge by waiting till January. Doing so is just not giving them a boost of confidence in you. It tells them that maybe you didn't have your act together. If the reason you were rejected the first time was due to unforced errors like a sloppy application or weaknesses, then you want to tighten it up and do a bulletproof app this time around. That means, one of the first two rounds.

The Duke adcom also wants you to interview again, even if you interviewed last season. It's an important input to their process and it would be to your advantage to do it. Doing so during the Open Interview season gives them all the more reason to believe that you're motivated and sincere. You can do the Open Interview and then apply in either Early Action or Round 1 and still get the brownie points.

Beyond that, the best advice we can give for a reapplicant to Duke: Be sure to show marked improvement in your profile. A full discussion of reapplicant strategies is beyond scope of this *SnarkStrategies Guide* however we do have a few specifics to offer. Even with what we're going to cover next, you may want to pick up our *Reapplicant's Guide* which would serve you well in mapping out your second attempt at a Duke MBA.

Any reapplicant, to any school, needs to show improvement. So the main problem with applying earlier in the season might be: You may feel that you don't have much to talk about.

This is especially true if you were on the waitlist and you didn't make it in. You probably were sending in updates to the Duke adcom about progress you made and changes at hand – stuff like new GMAT scores and maybe you took a class or you got this new assignment at work. If that's the case, don't sweat it. The baseline that Duke will be using to see "improvement" is last season's app.

Still, if your original application was Round 2 in January 2014, then that's not a whole lot of time to have made massive improvements to your profile. You do need to show *something* – you need to give the adcom reason to admit you. If last year's application didn't do it, then you can't just twiddle the bits on your essays and expect that to be enough. You must have evidence that your profile is actually stronger.

That's where the *Reapplicant Guide* can help.

We'll throw you a bone here though, because there's one key issue that reapplicants to Duke struggle with: The 25 Random Things essay.

We assume that in your first application, you dug deep and came up with the best list possible of the 25 things that are unique to you.

Most people don't have too much trouble coming up with 25 things the first time out. Maybe those last five were tough to think of. But 25 is doable. They put together a decent and interesting list. (Don't worry. If you've never done your 25 Things before, we're going to cover some dos and don'ts in a moment.)

If you're being asked to come up with *25 more* ... and you only have had less than a year between when you created the first one ... well, how is THAT supposed to work?

Good news, Brave Supplicant: You don't have to.

The reapplication to Duke needs to include an entire set of everything – but you only need to submit one new recommendation, and the 25 Things essay is optional.

This is clearly spelled out by Duke Admissions in their Application Instructions, which are available as a PDF within the online app system. Haven't read it? Maybe you should. It's eight pages of text in a very small font but it's got a wealth of information there. We're calling out the most important points in this *Guide* but you shouldn't be relying on us to digest this stuff. Anything the adcom says (at any school) is way more important than what a 'Snark might be asserting. Do yourself a favor and log on and read that puppy. It'll probably answer quite a bit of questions for you.

And if you're a reapplicant... no, you don't have to come up with a new list of 25 Things.

But guess what? We think that you should.

Or at least, you should radically re-do the list.

Unless your original list of 25 Things was the most polished work of art that you've ever created, then there's room for improvement. Ideally you'll want to have a couple of brand-new things at the beginning of this list.

Many adcom reviewers will be looking at your application fresh, without referring to last year's. It will be a new experience to read through your essays – mostly (there's always some exceptions, where an applicant is especially memorable – for either good, or not-so-good, reasons, and sometimes they might in fact remember someone from the prior year). In case they are looking at this year's 25 Things side by side with last year's, you want a clear indication that they're looking at something new. It's OK if the majority of your things are retained from last year's list; you want the first few to be new to the reader.

And, you should take the opportunity to redo the entire list. At minimum, we're guessing that there may be new ways to say what you originally said. And in some cases, we're certain that there might be items that should be deleted and new ones identified to replace them.

We'll go into lots of details on 25 Random Things next.

If you're in the reapplicant boat, we wish you luck – and we have high hopes that it will turn out well.

## Your Duke Essays

We mentioned earlier that it's important to be real in your Duke application. We touched on a common mistake BSers make: They write what they think they should. They say what they think the adcom wants to hear. This is basically the definition of "not real" when it comes to essay content. The place this falls apart the most is in Essay 2, when you're supposed to be talking about why you want to go to Duke, and the risk can be the greatest with the new alternative question for that essay.

The thing that trips people up is the phrasing: this is not meant as a posturing essay. This is meant as an honest, open discussion of the real reasons why you're interested in this school.

If you are too stiff and stilted in your language – and especially, if you do the first option for Essay 2 and you are coming from the place of trying to impress someone in a position of authority with the way you're writing – then your tone will be all off in the essay.

Instead, you need to be writing that essay from the perspective where they've asked it. That essay is where you back up the implicit claim that Duke is where you need to go to achieve the goals you've laid out in the short-answer responses.

Those short-answer responses? Those are going to give you the most grief.

The most difficult part of the Duke application is those three simple questions.

They're not even essays – in fact, it would be easier if they were. They're just so darn *short!*

By contrast with the friendly and open style that we're saying you need to have for Essay 2 – and for Essay 1, since it's a list of personal things about yourself – the way you write the responses to the career goals questions needs to be a little more buttoned up.

All your writing for Duke should be professional. But it doesn't all need to be so formal that it's alienating. Your objective with the two essays is to communicate a sense of who you are – to show some personality, even.

The short-answer responses are more clinical. You need to answer the question, and get out. You need them to be clean, and complete.

And you need to START your entire Duke application by figuring out the answers to those questions. Or else you'll be hosed when you start in on the essays (at least, Essay 2). Getting your career goals fully established is MANDATORY before you begin figuring out the rest of your Duke content.

Here's how to do it.

## Your Duke Career Goals

As with most bschools, the career goals must form the foundation of your pitch to Fuqua. They are really, truly important. And they are by far, with no competition, the key #1 place where Brave Supplicants fall down.

If you didn't get into bschool last year, it's almost guaranteed to be because your career goals were a mess. And/or your profile was out of whack, like unrealistic GMAT score or dismal GPA. And even if those flaws were present, it's likely that the career goals kinda sucked too. It's that common of a problem.

So let's make sure you don't end up in that category, Brave Supplicant. Let's see what we can do to help coach you to some winning set of career goals for Duke.

### *EssaySnark's career goals exercise*

This is an exercise we ask new clients to complete when we launch into a formal MBA admissions consulting engagement. This will serve you well as you begin to craft your answer to the Duke career goals question (it will actually serve you in tackling the goals question that any school asks, in any form or variety – that's why, if you're now a connoisseur of these *SnarkStrategies Guides*, you'll notice that we include it in almost every one).

> Please complete this fill-in-the-blank exercise. This is a good first step for you to develop your ideas for career goals, in order to demonstrate to the adcom what you want to do and why an MBA is essential:
>
> **1. "After I get my MBA I will be/do X"**
>
> Add as much detail as you can – job title, industry or niche, functional area, specialty, example companies to work for, geography, etc.
>
> *[Write your answer here. Go ahead. Nobody will look at it.]*
>
> _____
>
> _____
>
> _____
>
> _____

## 2. "My long term goal is to do Y"

Less detail needed, but must be clear and specific, and rational, given the s/t goal.

*[Write this one down, too.]*

_____

_____

_____

## 3. "An MBA from Duke is critical for me to achieve this because"

Solid reasons that point to the differentiation offered by Duke are critical here — you'll want to express how it will explicitly give you the skills you need for the short-term goal.

*[This is important. Use more space if you need to.]*

_____

_____

_____

_____

### 4. "Now is the right time for me to get an MBA because: "

A younger candidate would include a quick statement of why they feel they're ready, other candidates might describe how they need the MBA now to take advantage of the opportunities they see in their industry; all candidates should focus on career milestones, significant professional achievements, and other signs of "readiness" to show how you're at a point in your career where you will benefit from the MBA — this can be answered in a lot of different ways, so see what you can come up with on the "why now?" side.

*[This 'readiness' answer could be incorporated into Duke Essay 2 – it's not entirely mandatory to come through in the essays but it MUST come through implicitly in the application.]*

_____

_____

_____

_____

The short-term goal should have significant detail, and the bschool experience needs to be the setup for that (bschool should be positioned as the best means possible to prepare you for that s/t goal). The long-term goal needs much less detail but it needs to be logical and achievable, given the interim goals. You wouldn't want to position bschool as prep for the l/t goal, only the short-term one.

Yes, even though Duke hasn't explicitly asked for a "title" in their essay question, it wouldn't hurt to put one in. That type of specificity can take you far. It shows that you've put some thought into it, that you've researched the options, that you know the industry. These sorts of details truly cannot hurt you, and in many ways, they will help you stand out.

You should spend some time on this. What most people come up with their first time out is far from sufficient. You may even need to go off and do some research on your target industry and find out what types of jobs are available and what you'd be doing in them. Do some digging. Flesh this out. An off-the-cuff set of career goals will not help you get into the Fuqua MBA program.

## So what's a bad career goal?

Let's look at a few examples.

> "I want to become a leader in the financial services industry."

We see this all the time. Sorry folks. "Leader" is meaningless. And, believe it or not, so is "financial services." Much too broad. Are you talking about a big bank? A hedge fund? A mutual fund or other investment management company? Even insurance companies are often lumped into "financial services." This sentence is near-meaningless. It doesn't tell us anything about *what you want to do*.

Here's another one:

> "I want to be on the executive team of a multinational corporation."

Same problem. Sure, "executive team" has a little more specificity than "leader" however it still doesn't tell us *what you want to do*. (Note the theme?) And "multinational corporation" is just a blob of a term. What type of corporation? In which country? If you're interested in some type of international angle to your career, then you need to say that! This term is communicating next to nothing — except to say that maybe you haven't really put that much thought into it yet.

The other issue with both of these "bad" examples (probably) is timing. It's unrealistic to assume you'll be much of a "leader" — at least, not on a grand scale or anything — within the timeframe that Fuqua is asking you to present with these career goals. Nobody can see the future. Nobody knows what you'll be doing in 15 years. And yet that's how long it would take for most people to gain the experience, skills, and connections to actually become a CFO or what have you. It's highly unlikely you'll be rocking that boat within the timeframe expected in a "short/long-term goals" question from any school. So, saying you'll be on the ELT of a big conglomerate is a little unrealistic, probably.

Instead, you need to focus on literally what type of job you'll get right when you come out of Duke, and then, carve out a plan for how you'll progress from there, to perhaps another position, and at most, one more, which you'll identify as your long-term target. That final job that you present as your long-term goal should be within a reasonable timeframe. The foreseeable future. Like, maybe ten years from now, max (even that is not really "foreseeable" given how quickly things change in our lives and the world these days).

Keep in mind that most people are promoted maybe once every two years. If you consider your long-term goal to be in the five- to eight-year post-MBA timeframe, that will help you see (hopefully) what might be a realistic target to present for the adcom. **Given where you're at today in your career (level/role/title/responsibilities), what is a probable trajectory for you to end up in, say, the year 2025?**

If you need a little more space to capture your thinking on your long-term goal, go right ahead:

_____

_____

_____

_____

One exception where it might fly to tell the adcom that you'll be "CEO"? If you're going to be working in a family business after you graduate. If that's the case, then it's fine to say you're going to be taking over the whole show. You have different challenges than most people in presenting your goals (which are outside the discussion of this guide) however this could work in being realistic and believable.

What did we just say? Something about "realistic and believable"? Yes, that sounds good. This is something to make note of formally and officially. In fact, let's call it:

# Snarky Strategy #5

### Your career goals must be *believable* and *achievable*.

We've alluded to this already, with the comments about timeframe and what's feasible to accomplish in the long-term goal horizon that the school expects. The Duke adcom is really, truly going to look at your goals and see if they make sense. Is this a plan that you will be able to pull off? Is it do-able? Or more like a pipe dream?

An important takeaway here is: *Don't make stuff up.* The point of this exercise is not to present the most amazing, aggressive, flamboyant-sounding goals the school has ever seen. Actually, it's usually much more effective to present goals that are very standard, traditional, perhaps even a little run-of-the-mill.

Bschool candidates are always told that they have to stand out, that they have to differentiate themselves. Well guess what? The career goals essay is not the place to do this. You will differentiate yourself through the answers to the other questions. For the Duke short-answer questions, you don't have a choice; you must be rational, direct, and concise. And specific.

A few additional warnings:

- If you're looking to use bschool to make some **radical career change**, you have a bigger challenge. You need to show the adcom that you have transferable skills and are equipped to make the transition to the new field. This can be especially critical for those going in a dissimilar direction, e.g., IT guys wanting to go into finance. You'll need to show how you're ready to make this leap.

- Conversely, if you're not showing ENOUGH transition — if your stated **short-term goal is too similar** (or even identical) to what you are already currently doing in your job today — then you're not giving the adcom enough evidence of why you need an MBA. You should position yourself as ADVANCING, and then show how the MBA is the one main requirement that you need to get from A to B.

# A Snarky Caveat

The three most common mistakes with bschool career goals are:

- **They're too vague**

- **They're too ambitious**

- **They're too broad**

If your goals suffer from any of these sins, it's highly unlikely that Duke, or any top business school, will let you in.

- ***Too vague*** means saying you want to work in "financial services" or on an "executive team" or that you want to go into "international business." None of these are careers, they are concepts.

- ***Too ambitious*** is a goal that's written to impress the reader instead of being attainable for the candidate's actual skills and experience – often goals that involve starting a company/nonprofit/private equity fund fall into this category. It's fine to have an entrepreneurial goal, provided you lay the foundation appropriately for it.

- ***Too broad*** frequently happens when the applicant can't make up his mind and so he brings in multiple options of "I could do this or I might do that." While it could very well be true that you will pursue different options and paths once you're in the process of earning your MBA, it is usually a mistake to try and present all these different options to the adcom in the essays. There simply isn't room to provide an appropriate level of detail on more than one possible career path.

Duke tends to reward candidates who express confidence and conviction, who sound like they have an honest-to-goodness action plan. Sure, your life may take you in a different direction once the wheels are in motion. What the bschool folks want to see is that you're mature and responsible, that you know how to take control of your life and that you're able to make your own success. A well-crafted set of essays will communicate this.

In a nutshell: Keeping that ***realistic and believable*** guideline in mind as you refine your goals should help you avoid these problems.

One more note: Sometimes people actually make their career goals *too specific*. Usually EssaySnark is trying to cajole our clients in the opposite direction – typically their goals are not specific enough – however sometimes, we get a Brave Supplicant who takes this to an extreme. Case in point? One year we had a client state to us her long-term goal that she wants to be CMO (Chief Marketing Officer) of Apple.

Why is this a problem? Well, for starters, it implies that the Brave Supplicant thinks a little highly of herself, to assume that she's going to qualify for this cream-of-the-crop job. But the other issue: There's only one of these jobs in the whole wide world. Apple has just one CMO, and you can bet that there're a whole lotta people who'd love to be it.

(Please don't use the fact that current Apple CEO Tim Cook went to Duke to think that this is a good goal to use for your Fuqua application.)

# A Snarky Caveat

## We're serious about the *achievable* thing.
## It's got to be achievable for YOU.

Sure, you very well may end up being Chief Marketing Officer at Apple in a couple decades or so – maybe. But you won't be there in the standard five to eight years post-MBA that the adcom has in mind with the long-term goal time horizon. And worse, you're painting yourself into a bit of a box to say that this is the one and only job you aspire to.

Instead, broaden your goal out, either by position ("a senior-level position in marketing") and/or by company ("at a leading company such as Apple or ..."). Be sure to name more than one company. Demonstrate your intent through a well-thought out plan.

You likely won't have room to cover all of this with your Duke short-answer responses, but you can use them in other applications. And, importantly, the fact that you have worked through all these details will be clear to the reader when she goes through your Duke Essay 2 – and you can bet that this stuff will come up when you go to interview.

We heard an author once say that she knew her readers could still feel all the pieces of her characters' stories that she had to cut out during editing, that the process of constructing it and then scaling it back was what gave it power.

If you take the time to map out your goals with these exercises, you will have more confidence. Your writing will have more conviction. Your essay will resonate for the adcom.

Before we get too much farther, we want to offer our recommendation for all your essays – not just Duke, but everyone.

Duke's essay instructions say that you have to fit each of Essay 1 and 2 into two pages maximum, 1.5-line spacing, 10-point font minimum (that's two pages per essay).

# A Snarky Caveat

### Even though they allow smaller, please use an 11-point (or larger) font if you possibly can.

You hopefully already know that you should choose a standard font face like Times New Roman or Arial (we prefer Times, typically). The thing with the font size is, it's just really hard to read when the essays are written in smaller fonts. It also makes it look like you didn't do the work to edit yourself.

Part of the task of the writer is to be clear and concise – obviously Duke is *forcing* you to do that with the short-answer questions on goals. And for good reason; people often wax poetic on longer essays, and that's defeating the purpose of communicating your plans for yourself.

Duke is remarkably generous with its length limits on essays 1 and 2. We would suggest that you try to not outstay your welcome. Writing – and editing – your work down so that it easily fits on the two 1.5-spaced pages, at a decent font size, would be much appreciated by your adcom reader.

Are you ready to actually write some essays, then?

## Duke Short-Answer Questions

Each of these three subquestions that Duke has asked you must stand on its own. This breaking-down of a career goals essay into its subparts makes it even more challenging to get your message across to the adcom. These individual questions don't allow you to go in-depth on any responses. You're going to be hard pressed to fit in everything that EssaySnark is going to tell you needs to be in here. But believe us, it is possible – maybe not simple, but possible. This is why application development takes time.

You'll start out with a whole bunch more content than you can ever fit in. You'll need to spend a lot of time combing through and filtering out and refining the language you're using. That's where the work comes in. If it was just about writing out a paragraph or so on what you want to do, it would be a snap.

Instead, you need to shoehorn your answer into *literally 250 characters for each response.* Did you catch that? We said 250 CHARACTERS. *Not "words".*

The online application will cut off your answer after the allotted number of characters. You literally have no other choice but to write a brief response.

### *Constructing Your Short-Answer Responses*

First: You have read through the entire Duke application, right? Because they have a question in the Program Information section of the app that asks you to name your Future Career Focus. It's got a dropdown box – two, actually – listing out all sorts of industries, like energy and healthcare and consulting. You can specify "Entrepreneurship" and "Information Technology" if you want to do a software startup. Or whatever.

Before you start writing your answer to this first short-response question, you should probably take a gander at that list and figure out what you intend to choose there.

You could fill in the "Other" field in that section if you had to, but we'd recommend sticking with the predefined values in the dropdown if you can.

OK, now that you know what you want to do... Go back to the exercises that you completed from the earlier section of this *Guide* and see what you came up with.

The first question – What are your short term goals, post-MBA? That one should be easy. Most people have a sense for what they want to do immediately after they get the MBA (or they do, after they have gone through our little exercise).

And you hopefully now have a good answer to the long-term goal question too, now that we filled you in on what the schools want to see there.

The place you're likely to get hung up is the last question. What's your backup plan?

What you want to do here is present a viable alternative *short-term goal* that would help you to still achieve this long-term thing that you've laid down.

The biggest problem we see is people name another path that has either nothing to do with the long-term goal they originally cited – it would take them in an entirely different direction. Or, it has nothing to do with where they're at now and the MBA.

As an example:

You probably will have a hard time explaining why you want to go into consulting now, in order to later start your company – and then claim that if you can't get a job as a consultant, you'll just start the company.

That really doesn't fly. If your whole proposition is that you need the MBA in order to become a consultant, and you need that experience before you can begin a company... why would you all of a sudden be ready to launch the company if you hit a roadblock on finding a job as a consultant?

Does not compute.

This is not an easy exercise, we admit. The Duke adcom knows what they're doing in forcing you to think through these options. And this is another reason why we're not going to sit here and suggest a bunch of ideas for you. These needs to be YOUR plans for your future – not ours. Plus, if we listed out a bunch of alternate paths here, then the Duke admissions team would be getting a whole bunch of answers that all looked suspiciously alike. And that would help nobody.

Besides have an alternate path that's not rational in light of the Plan A that they're naming for themselves, another mistake that people make is their goals are just too generic.

Maybe it's fine to simply state in the first answer that you want to be a strategy consultant. The problem with that is that *everybody* wants to be a strategy consultant. Ho hum. Boring.

There's no problem with that intrinsically – after all, it is what bschool is for. Duke sends a lot of people into consulting, so they're OK with that.

But it's not taking full advantage of your (albeit limited) opportunity to share parts of yourself.

Some ideas on what you might do to further expand and extend and enhance your statements of goals are:

- Make them personal – reference something about your motivations, interests, or rationale for making this big jump

- Tie them to your past – mention your existing career (in a very concise way) that hooks the goals to your existing experience

- Optionally, make mention of Duke and say something – briefly! – about how that plays in

These two ideas are most relevant for your answer to the first question, around the short-term goal. You might also want to do that in the long-term goal answer too, but remember that your job with the MBA application is to show how your current experience, plus the Duke MBA, will be the proper setup to the short-term goal. You should not be positioning the Duke MBA as the needed preparation to your long-term goal. Your long-term goal is way off down the road. You need to leverage all the resources at your disposal during your MBA experience to be prepared for the immediate next step after bschool. Don't clutter up your thinking with how you're going to use the MBA to prepare for a much-later goal that you can't even hardly envision just yet.

If you are talking too much in the essays about how you need the MBA in order to be ready for your long-term goal, then what you're doing is talking yourself out of that as a long-term goal. You could be inadvertently making the reader believe that you really want to be doing the long-term thing now, right away, immediately after you graduate. Getting stuff out of sequence like this can muddle your messaging and make the whole thing more complicated to present clearly.

Once you've got a rationalized view of Duke MBA → S/T goal → L/T Goal, then you need to step back and look at that long-term goal, and identify an alternate path that would also help you get there. This is where you can demonstrate maturity, and critical thinking, and flexibility. This is where the adcom can actually test if you *need* the MBA – and if you're committed to your future plans. The long-term goal should not change; you should be able to come up with another means for you to achieve it.

Whatever you say in response to these questions, the goals you specify should be a natural outgrowth of what you've done to date. You can completely switch direction and pursue some entirely new goals, but it should be fairly obvious why you want to go do this new thing, based on how you present it, and your background. The adcom reader shouldn't be left scratching her head after reading it.

Remember that the adcom has your resume; you don't need to stuff in all of that into these short-answer questions. You can also potentially mention some of it in Essay 2 as needed to fill in the gaps (Essay 1 is not typically the best place for professional stuff). These first short-answer responses are not the entirety of your pitch; you will be evaluated on everything, and how all the pieces fit together.

However, whatever answer you give in these short-response questions shouldn't be such a radical departure from everything you've done before that we are skeptical in seeing how you'll pull it off. You can present a big career jump in the essays – you can tell the adcom how you want to go do something quite different from what you've done before – but you need to establish some continuity in terms of how you're prepared for the challenges you'll face. The best essays show how you have had a plan and you have been executing on it. You don't want to come across as an accidental traveler. The elements of your past must fit together into where you say you want to go in the future. This messaging and fitting-together of the elements is up to you. Just don't toss out something so unrelated to your past that it makes no sense for how you'll get there. The adcom wants to see what your thinking was in choosing the path that you have.

## Essay 1: 25 Random Things

1. The list of 25 Things that you put together should be fun to write. That should be evident in what you say and how you say it.

2. We recommend sticking with topics outside of work. It's fine to mention some professional achievement if it's big and significant — but if it's already on your resume, we're not sure it belongs on this list.

3. In almost all cases, we suggest listing things that you have not mentioned elsewhere in your application.

4. Our best advice on learning what types of things should go in this list is to read the samples that the adcom posted on the Duke website. You should also read the Random Things that some of the student profiles include.

5. Most Random things should be a sentence. Two is fine. Going much more than that — especially if it's extending into paragraph-length — is not good.

6. An abbreviated phrase is great.

7. You'll want to figure out an order for your list. Don't just dump everything out. Even though it's "random" you should still design the sequence so that it makes sense.

8. Grouping like items together is often a good strategy.

9. A chronological sequence also works well.

10. Pay attention to the item that you end on. It should have some "oomph." Avoid using downer statements as your final entry; nothing about how your best friend when you were little was a goldfish and it died. Stick with something more uplifting or positive or success-focused as your finale, if you can.

11. Remember that ALL of the entries need to be focused on you. It's fine to mention a friend or family member but keep all comments centered on you personally. (This is a common mistake.)

12. If you include the names of songs, artists, books, or movies, then it's best if they're ones the reader will be familiar with. Avoid obscure references.

13. This can be a great place to mention your hobbies.

14. Extracurricular activities are also perfectly appropriate.

15. You can go back as far as you like. There's no timeframe or restrictions with your list.

16. It MUST be only two pages total. Pay attention to the formatting requirements.

17. (And remember what we said about the font size.)

18. Even though you can write in phrases, you need to pay attention to grammar. And spelling. And punctuation. Avoid sentence fragments, and be careful about items that are unrelated getting lumped together for no valid reason.

19. Be sensitive to TMI ("too much information"). While the adcom wants to know about you as a person, it's totally possible to get *too* personal. Don't reveal stuff that would make your reader uncomfortable. Remember, they're trying to get to know you. If you've had really awful things happen in your life, then they might not belong in this list. It'll be up to you to evaluate.

20. Remember that this is an application to a professional program. Don't get too risque.

21. Even though this seems like a fun and almost trivial exercise, it's super important – and it's unlikely you'll be able to come up with the perfect list during your first time out. You'll want to leave this aside and come back to it.

22. A good exercise if you get stuck: Ask your best friend what he or she thinks is the most interesting thing about you. Ask your mom for a childhood memory.

23. Keep everything you write as specific as possible. Don't say that "People like me" unless you're able to back it up with an example of some kind. Remember the advice to "show, don't tell" - the best items on the list will be concrete, and vivid.

24. Don't be afraid to brag a little. If you've done something awesome, share it! Just don't be obnoxious about it, and make sure that everything you cite is credible.

25. The Duke admissions team really likes this essay. You'll find out why as you work out your list. Have fun with it! It's the best MBA application out there.

## Essay 2: Why Duke?

This year, they shifted things a bit by introducing a new alternative prompt that you could tackle for Essay 2 instead of the original since prompt they've had, about what would you tell your friends as to why you want to go to Duke.

Both of this year's Essay 2 prompts are actually asking the same thing. We believe that a main reason that they introduced a choice for this question is to allow for some variety in the adcom readers' lives. It must get a little tedious when everyone is responding to the exact-same set of questions and the essays start to sound a lot alike. While we have seen some interesting answers and good essays for Duke Essay 2, by and large, people end up talking about a lot of similar stuff.

With either of these questions, you really need to do a lot of research about the school and the opportunity that it offers before you can even start to touch the essay.

In terms of which question to use, well, we are going to make a bold statement and say that it could be an advantage to do the second essay, about the Duke values – *provided you execute well.* That alternate question also has some hidden gotchas and it would be very possible to completely step in it when trying to craft a good answer. The biggest risk with it is that it's phrased in a forward-looking way; you're supposed to talk about completely imagined stuff that has not happened yet. This style of essay question is common to schools like Kellogg and now MIT, and they can be very difficult to write – and sometimes people overstep the boundaries.

It doesn't help to be too broad-reaching in all the amazing stuff you say you're going to do while at Duke. Instead, you need to ground everything that you say in that essay in something tangible from your past, that shows how you are in fact the type of person to go pursue that and achieve it. You would need to do this if you choose the first option to write about, too, but the risk isn't so great that you'll fly off into the clouds and lose track of reality with that one.

The other problem with the second option – which we see as a massive opportunity for you – is that just like with the Defining Principles at UC Berkeley-Haas, these six Team Fuqua Principles are pretty opaque. While some of them are easy enough to understand, others are just not all that easy to grok. What is "impactful stewardship" after all? You will need to demonstrate a keen understanding of whichever principle that you choose to write about – and sometimes people's understanding of such things are just off. And that of course is where the opportunity comes in for you: If you do a good job of expressing your appreciation for the specific Principle that you're presenting, then it's likely to be much more compelling than anything you might share if you had answered the former essay question about friends and family.

We don't want to discourage you to do the friends and family question. There are some possible potholes that you might encounter with that one, too, which we will lay out in detail here. Let's start by looking at each of these prompts and offer some directives on them, so you can start to juggle out which you feel might be best for you.

## *Duke Second Essay Prompt #1*

This is the same question they have had for a few years now, and it goes like this:

> *When asked by your family, friends, and colleagues why you want to go to Duke, what do you tell them? Share the reasons that are most meaningful to you.*

First we have to point out something that's maybe a little subtle, but at the same time, so revealing: It's the way that Duke Admissions asks their questions.

They ask you to "share" - not even "tell us." The language that they use gives insights into the culture. "Share" is such a collaborative word.

In line with Duke's very personal approach to the essay questions, this prompt specifically says to "Share the reasons that are most meaningful to you" about why you want to go to Duke. And whoa, they give you two pages to do it in. Double-spaced pages, but two pages nonetheless. Exceedingly generous.

Next, we are going to give you a heads-up on one of the questions that Duke asked way back in 2010:

> *Why Duke? (If you are interested in a specific concentration, joint degree, clubs or activities, please discuss how you would contribute to these in this essay.)*

You can basically use that prompt instead of the "friends and family" one to guide what you want to say.

That being said, make sure to write specific to the question being asked. We've already given you the most important advice if you choose this prompt (and all prompts, but especially this one): **Answer the question.** Don't be stiff. Write it as if you're literally answering the question to your family or friends. The worst is when someone has this overly formal and almost pompous answer writing what they think they're supposed to say.

Remember that nothing in the essay question asks about your background. While it can often be relevant and appropriate to give some context to your goals and why you want to go to

Duke, you probably should not go off on some tangent about your past experiences and career successes. That's not how to start off with this essay. The adcom has your resume for that. You can use a story like that as backup, but we're not sure that it works too well to begin with that.

Instead, start with your very best, most important, most compelling reason that you've discovered for why you want to go to Duke. In other words, *answer the question.* Phrase it in the way that they've asked for it; talk about in the context of how you've had these conversations with others in your life. Share something that would be relevant in such a conversation. (And please don't say "Because Duke is ranked well" - that's just too superficial). Think about your actual honest-to-goodness reasons for why this school appeals to you, and use those.

This is why it's important to have done all that research we've been encouraging you to do. This is why you want to go visit the school in advance of applying. This is why you need to be networking with Fuqua people.

Besides expanding on what literally your goals are beyond the limited answer you gave earlier, this particular question lets you also explain why you're ready to pursue those goals. You can weave in an example or two (or three, or four) from your own life in a way that demonstrates why the Duke MBA is the right next step. But if you try to re-use an essay written for another school's goals question, it'll be pretty obvious straight away.

In fact, we have an easy test for this one: You should be able to tell that it's written for Duke Essay 2 even if there's no question posted at the top – and taking it even further, *you should be able to instantly tell that it was written for this particular prompt*. (You should always post the question at the top of your essay though – this is even more important now when there's two choices you could be answering. But it should be obvious which question it's for even without that.) We can't imagine a situation where someone answering the other option for Essay 2 could end up writing an essay that seems like it's a fit for this prompt, but we can definitely see where the opposite could happen. If you're not clear in your opening about the direction you're setting for yourself and where you're headed as a writer, then you could introduce some confusion in the mind of your reader.

The most effective way to do this is to weave in the question itself into the first part of your essay, and to write it in a way that proves you're telling your family and friends these things. You wouldn't go off on some dissertation about your career history if a buddy asked why you want to go to bschool. You *might* reference your background - "Because of my experience in such-and-such..." – but you wouldn't belabor it. You'd simply answer the question, based on what he'd asked you. Do that, in your intro to this essay.

It's still relevant and useful to provide some context or foundation for why the MBA from Duke is right for you, and there's plenty of ways you can feed that information in. You might want to give some specific example that summarizes or highlights the strengths of your career and communicates more than can be seen with a quick glance at your resume. You might want to showcase the wins, the turning points, or the major successes. Perhaps you could mention some big achievements and where they brought you. Drill down into one of those key moments, then use it as a springboard to say, "Because of that, I'm ready to take advantage of the Duke MBA in this way" and then name some specific thing about Duke that gets you excited.

Obviously you need to line these items up. You can't just toss out an experience from your past and then name some random thing about Duke. These need to be well integrated. This is where you use those critical thinking skills that you've so finely developed in your life.

When you're staring at a blank screen, it may seem that two pages is just so much to fill. This essay isn't actually going to be that long – it's only about 800 words, maybe. If you are feeling stumped on what to say, then here's some possible angles for you to explore – and remember, we ALWAYS suggest doing an outline first, before starting to write especially with a rather unstructured question like this one, you'll want to get your core ideas down before you start your draft.

Here's some suggestions on angles you might cover – these are suggestions only! There's lots of directions you can go in. Essay 2 is where you impart your love for Duke. This is where you pull out all the stops and talk with enthusiasm about what you know about the school and why those attributes are important to you.

This is where:

- You impress the adcom with all the efforts you've made to research the program, reach out to the students and alumni, interact with the admissions team, and engage with the Duke community

- You articulate your understanding for what Duke is about in a way that shows how you will leverage same in your own educational process

- You state why now is the time for the MBA, based on how you're ready to take advantage of your past experiences and make the move in this new direction. Why are you ready to go do this new thing you want to do? This can come through in a gazillion ways, but it can certainly be addressed in the essay.

Hmmm.... That list actually is equally appropriate for guidance for option 2 of Essay 2 also.

Either way, this essay should have *specifics*. With the first option in particular, the Duke adcom is pointing out that you should come to campus, or to meet the admissions team as they travel the world, or do *something* to learn about their school. Do some networking, ask some questions. Take the time to find out if Duke is really the right place for you, and then reflect on the reasons why – and put it down in your essay.

# A Snarky Caveat

If you visited campus or attended an info session – *tell them about it!* Include the month of your interaction in Essay 2 Prompt 1 (include the year, too, if it was not recent). Name some names.

The way to make a strong pitch to Duke or any school is to include specifics in your arguments. Nowhere is this more important than in Duke Essay 2.

In all honesty, this essay should be easy to write, at least, compared to others you have to deal with for different schools. Focus in on the tone, write in a natural voice, and include specifics about literally *why do you want to go to Duke?* And you should be in very good shape. Please make sure that you're selecting this prompt for a good reason, though. Just because it's easier to write does not mean that it's the one you should do. Often, the harder essay questions result in better essays (often, but not always; we're looking at you, MIT).

# Snarky Strategy #6

The most important consideration with Essay 2 Prompt 1 is that you are communicating in natural language. This essay should sound like you when you read it out loud.

Our best advice if you choose the first prompt for Essay 2? Present your content as if you're trying to make a friend. Don't write to impress. While the tone should still be formal and professional, beware of sounding too stiff – and definitely try to avoid sounding like you're trying to impress someone.

How do you test it?

Read your essay out loud. Harvard's admissions director even suggests that you read your draft for their open-ended question out loud, to yourself, standing in front of a mirror. You might want to try that with this essay, too. As you do it, listen to yourself.

Is that how you speak when you talk to your friends? Does the voice that you hear saying the words sound like you?

If you stumble on any words – or if they don't feel natural coming out of your mouth – then they don't belong. Change them.

This essay should have your enthusiasm pouring forth off the page. That doesn't mean you should be tossing out ridiculous saccharine-laden adjectives and writing like a 14-year-old-girl talking to her besties. It does mean that your genuine excitement for Duke should be easily and readily apparent.

Yes, revision will be necessary.

The alternate to this original Essay 2 prompt may not be quite so easy to write – which is again another reason why we think that you should probably try to write it.

## Duke Second Essay Prompt #2

Here's the behemoth of a question:

> *The Team Fuqua community is as unique as the individuals who comprise it. Underlying our individuality are a number of shared ideas and principles that we live out in our own ways. Our students have identified and defined 6 "Team Fuqua Principles" that we feel are the guiding philosophies that make our community special. At the end of your 2 years at Fuqua, if you were to receive an award for exemplifying one of the 6 Principles listed below, which one would it be and why? Your response should reflect the research you have done, your knowledge of Fuqua and the Daytime MBA program and experience, and the types of activities and leadership you would engage in as a Fuqua student.*

> 1. ***Authentic Engagement:*** *We care and we take action. We each make a difference to Team Fuqua by being ourselves and engaging in and supporting activities about which we are passionate.*
>
> 2. ***Supportive Ambition:*** *We support each other to achieve great things, because your success is my success. The success of each individual member of Team Fuqua makes the whole of Team Fuqua better.*
>
> 3. ***Collective Diversity:*** *We embrace all of our classmates because our individuality is better and stronger together.*
>
> 4. ***Impactful Stewardship:*** *We are leaders who focus on solutions to improve our communities both now and in the future. We aren't satisfied with just maintaining the status quo.*
>
> 5. ***Loyal Community:*** *We are a family who looks out for each other. Team Fuqua supports you when you need it the most.*
>
> 6. ***Uncompromising Integrity:*** *We internalize and live the honor code in the classroom and beyond. We conduct ourselves with integrity within Fuqua, within Duke, and within all communities of which we are a part.*

Wow. OK. What do you do with *that?* Let's see if we can break this down for you.

First and foremost, we need to call your attention to the "Team Fuqua" thing. This has been an everpresent part of the Duke MBA community for a very long time. (First tip: You probably should figure out how to pronounce "Fuqua." ☺ ) You'll notice that it's referenced in the first question, too. What does this mean and what are these Principles about?

We believe that these Principles have their origin in some equally-dense and hard-to-tease-apart concepts relating to another buzzword at Fuqua: the *leader of consequence.* You can find references to this leader of consequence thing on their website but it's been moved to the side in the past few years; it used to be front-and-center, such that you had to answer an essay question about it. So what in heck does THAT mean?

This is what then-Dean Blair Sheppard said in an interview in 2008:

> ```
> Our mission since 1984 is to teach and conduct
> research; to create leaders of consequence. And one
> of our values is to be consistent about our mission.
> We follow the three dualities.
>
> Every student at Fuqua:
>
> 1. We expect to be a great member of the team and be
> able to lead, when it is their turn to lead;
>
> 2. We expect to be a really brilliant disciplinarian
> and a globalist;
>
> 3. We want to be really, really smart and real.
>
> It's this juxtaposition of the opposites that is at
> the core of who we are.
> ```

OK, that probably didn't help you much, at least not on an initial reading. We encourage you to come back to this as you are working through your essays. It's possible that some of this may click into place for you as you are delving the depths of your own material in answer to the question.

Here's a more accessible resource in helping you to understand Team Fuqua in action, written by a member of the Executive MBA program in 2013:

http://blogs.fuqua.duke.edu/weekend-mba/2013/07/05/%E2%80%9Cteam-fuqua%E2%80%9D-is-not-just-a-slogan?category=student-life

That communicates it well. You'll want to be on the lookout for ways that Team Fuqua expresses itself to you in your own interactions with the school community. Remember to take notes on these! You'll need them – not just for this essay but for your interview as well.

Our guidelines for your approach to this option for Duke Essay 2:

1. This is obvious since it's stated in the question, but you have to pick just one of these six Principles to focus on. There are going to be plenty of story ideas that you come up with that could potentially fit more than one Principle. That's fine, and maybe even a positive, but you need to focus on one and only one in the essay – and you need to have enough sophistication in how you talk about it, and present your story, such that it's clear that you can perceive how that Principle is unique amongst its peers. If the story you tell is too muddy, diffuse, or broad, then it's not going to be a good support system for the Principle that you have selected as your answer.

2. If an idea for an essay immediately jumped out at you when you first read the list – for example, on the Loyal Community one, because you've got this great story about how you stuck by someone when something went sour on a project, and you faced the consequences of taking the blame instead of throwing the other person under the bus, then that might be a great story to tell in your essay. However for most people, we do not recommend choosing your essay topic based on choosing one of the Principles.

3. Instead, a better approach is to create an inventory of your best stories, and dissect and analyze them, to see which demonstrates any of the Principles, and then to select the one that is not only the strongest fit to one particular Principle, but also the one which adds the most value in rounding out your profile.

4. Therefore, one of your strategies in figuring out which story to tell in this essay is to look at the gaps and weaknesses in your profile, and see how you can shore those up.

   - If you are a non-traditional candidate like a Teach for America alum, and/or your quant skills are not well represented in the standard stats of GMAT and GPA, then perhaps there's a story you can use from the workplace, that shows you in action utilizing that keen analytical mind of yours.

   - Or if you're coming from Wall Street, where there's a built-in perception of the stereotype of someone who is rather out for himself and looking towards the bottom line in all things, then perhaps you have a story of rescuing a kitten from a tree. You could use that to show your softer side. (This is obviously a made-up example, for demonstration purposes only. Your story needs to be a little bigger than kitten-rescuing.)

   - If you have entrepreneurial goals, then you might want to find a good story to show how you understand risk and are willing to take a well-considered chance, as a means to pursue your goals.

The story that you present in this essay should be multi-dimensional. Not only will you want it to accurately reflect the Principle that you have chosen to discuss, but you also (ideally) will want it to communicate new parts of your profile that will fill in the gaps, or smooth the rough edges, in the other elements of your background as depicted on your application.

Oh wait. There's a question in the back of the room.

"EssaySnark, why are we talking about stories to tell in this essay? The essay instructions say to talk about Fuqua."

Good catch, Brave Supplicant! This essay needs to do both.

As we warned previously, the difficulty with this essay is if you write the whole thing about what you will do during your time at Fuqua, then it can come across as a little hyped up. Or sometimes a lot.

You definitely do want to present those items in the essay. You'll want to talk about the classes or the clubs or whatever other aspects of Fuqua that excite you – provided you do so in the context of where you'll make a contribution.

That's at least half the essay. But the best part to PROVE that all the future-focused stuff you're spouting is actually going to happen if they admit you, is to reference similar stuff from your background that demonstrates the selected Principle.

So, say you are going to tell the adcom about your interest in NetImpact. Lots of people talk about that in their Duke essays, and it can be perfectly appropriate for you to do so. You'll need to go beyond the surface level with what you say; you can't simply say you want to be in the club and do their events; you need to explore how you would dive in and make a contribution. And you'd want to present that NetImpact reference as backup in support of a statement that you feel you would qualify for the Impactful Stewardship Principle.

Sidebar: This is kind of obvious stuff; there's going to be lots of people naming that particular Principle and citing some NetImpact interest in support of it. Just a caution.

Anyway, say you write a paragraph or maybe two about all that stuff. All that does is entice a yawn from your reader. Remember, actions speak louder than words. It's easy to throw out broad and ambitious claims about how you will spend your two years on campus and all the great impact you intend to have. That's pretty much expected, in terms of how people write a lot of MBA admissions essays.

What will set you apart is if you show *that you already embody the Principle that you're talking about, and you want to go to Fuqua as a way to expand upon it.*

And the way you do THAT is by presenting some evidence. You map out a quick story from your past where you showed Impactful Stewardship in some other context or organization. It doesn't have to be a formal non-profit volunteer experience, though it certainly could be.

Also, sometimes we caution people against talking up too many school activities or interests that are wholly unrelated to their stated future career goals. As an example, when we see someone touting the NetImpact stuff in their essays, and also how they want to serve on a non-profit board, and volunteer for some poverty program... then we look at their past, and their future, to make sure that these things are mutually reinforcing. It's totally fine for a stereotypical finance candidate to want to spend his time in bschool engaged in such activities, but if the balance is off, then it can raise questions. An always-skeptical adcom reader may assume that the BSer is hyping up these do-gooder activities as an attempt to sound good. It's too transparent of a ploy to say what you think you're supposed to say. There has to be continuity between what you say you want to do at Fuqua, and what you've actually already in real life been doing in the somewhat recent past.

# A Snarky Caveat

## The biggest risk with Duke Essay 2 Option 2 is that you come across as posturing.

It's too easy to make stuff up for this question, and if everything you present is just a nice idea, but not tied down to actual reality, then it can come across as disingenuous.

Our advice for coming up with ideas on the Fuqua draft is to make some lists.

You could do these one at a time, or you could try to brainstorm them all together. We recommend the former, since it'll be easier to isolate out which of your candidate examples might work best for a specific Principle, but you can handle this any way you like. We also suggest repeating this exercise at least three times over the course of as many days or even longer. It's going to surprise you how your subconscious starts to kick in with some nuggets of ideas, the longer you allow it to churn through this problem you're handing over to it.

This more generic "leadership" brainstormer is a good foundation exercise to start with:

### EssaySnark's brainstorming exercise for new clients

[Based on an actual assignment we give when starting an engagement.]

> As another step in developing your application theme, a useful exercise is to brainstorm about your major accomplishments. Haas wants to learn about you through your achievements and what you've done in your life. Where you've focused your energies and attention, and the impact you've had in the world (even on a small stage), will communicate volumes to the adcom. Getting an "inventory" of your major wins and significant life experiences will give you a sense of what to work from in creating your strategy.
>
> Put together a simple list of, say, your five (or six, or seven) most important achievements.
>
> **It's not recommended to write full essays for the purpose of this exercise.** This is about getting some ideas down, not in starting to

write the actual essays. People often get attached to a draft if they write it all out; it can be hard to redirect and start over. If you start to write a lot about one achievement, then stop. For the purpose of this exercise, it's best to just capture your key ideas. Make a list, that's all we're looking for. Since this is just for you, a bunch of backstory or explanation is not needed. That can come later, as you flesh the ideas out to a real essay. For now, just get the gist of each one; you shouldn't have to dig through a bunch of words to find the core of the achievement or event.

These achievements can be taken from literally any area of your life — the classroom, team projects, internships, community engagement with volunteering, extracurriculars from school, sports, even personal things like overcoming illness or dealing with parents' divorce or whatever. Lay it all out on a piece of paper. Anything is fair game at this stage. You should not edit yourself in terms of where these items come from in your life, nor need you worry about how current or ancient history they might be. When you go to create your essays, you'll mostly want to cover what you've done in the past three or four years, but for the purposes of this exercise, you can include anything at all of importance to you.

Where were the pivot-points in your life? Where did the track diverge and you started moving in a new direction?

Where did people stand up and applaud at something awesome that you did?

What does your mother brag to her friends about?

When thinking of professional accomplishments, try to identify ones where you met a tangible goal ("completed a project two weeks early", "passed an industry exam and received a professional certification", etc.), or specifically, achievements where your efforts made a direct contribution to your team, the customer, or the overall company in ways that can be measured ("reduced costs by 10%", "made the customer so happy that they bought another $100k product from us", etc.).

Here's a video from a few years back by Darden's Director of Admissions with a great idea on how to identify some of these more recent pivotal experiences or moments:

http://www.youtube.com/watch?v=dujl_GT6Uxo

Finally, if you're stuck on this: Force yourself to come up with ideas by doing a timed writing exercise. The way it works is this:

> 1. Set yourself up in a quiet place with a pen and a notepad.
>
> 2. At the top of the page, write in big block letters: MY MOST SIGNIFICANT ACCOMPLISHMENTS ARE.
>
> 3. Get a kitchen timer. Set it for five minutes.
>
> 4. Put the pen on the paper and start writing — and don't let yourself stop.
>
> Keep that pen moving until the timer goes off. It doesn't matter if you're writing about the topic at first — you could even begin by writing "I have no idea what to write." Just force yourself to write, don't worry about punctuation and spelling, nobody's going to see it. Keep going for the entire five minutes. Don't let the pen stop moving on the page.
>
> Nothing come of it? Give yourself a minute, get a cup of coffee, sit back down and do it again. Maybe change the prompt at the top of the page this time: WHAT AM I MOST PROUD OF? or WHERE HAVE I HAD AN IMPACT ON OTHERS?
>
> You may feel a little silly doing this exercise, but people are often surprised at what comes up — it's a way to force the subconscious mind into action, and sometimes it spits up some real gems!

A variation of that brainstorming exercise could look like this:

- Take each of the six Fuqua Principles one by one, and tease apart its essence. Select two or three words – nouns, adjectives or verbs – that captures that essence. Do a separate time brainstorming session around each group of words (one at a time, six times total).

The trick with this is to not just repeat the keywords of the Principle, but to find synonyms that carry more meaning for you, and then brainstorm around that.

So for "Engagement" you could rephrase it as "Get involved" - simpler, more accessible language is sometimes helpful for this. Then you write at the top of the page, "What are the best examples from my life where I have gotten involved?" Or even better, "What is the best example from work where I've gotten involved?" where you're specific on the context.

You may end up identifying the same examples for multiple Principles, which is OK at this stage, but you'll want to pick a lane when you go to write it up in the essay. The Principle that you're trying to demonstrate should be crystal clear and obvious to the reader, even if it wasn't named in the essay.

Tip: That's one way to test if you're there yet: Edit your draft to remove the actual Principle you're writing about, and hand it to someone who's never read any versions of this essay from you before. See if they can articulate the trait or quality that you're trying to convey. There's little chance they'll literally name the Principle as defined by Fuqua, but they should at least be in the same ballpark; they should hopefully name one or two of the synonyms for this Principle that you came up with during your initial brainstormers.

## *Personal or professional content?*

- Either personal or professional stories could work for this essay. If you select a professional story, then hopefully it's one that is interesting and impactful. You don't want to have an example of you simply doing your job. It needs to demonstrate how you went above and beyond the norm in this circumstance. The best stories of accomplishment show a *contribution* or in some other way are able to demonstrate impact (and this could fit many of the Principles). In relating the experience in your essay, there should be a "before" and an "after" state apparent from the story: You were faced with a specific challenge or problem to solve, you did XYZ, and then the outcomes were this. There's other ways to do it, but that template usually communicates what you need to communicate.

- We can also see how a personal story might work for this essay. This might be something about a personal challenge, or a crisis, dilemma, or setback, such as being laid off, a health issue, losing a parent, an accident, or possibly a story about significant weight loss or other personal triumph. This is not mandatory, but sharing something personal with the adcom (done in an appropriate, professional, and relevant way) can illuminate elements of your background for them and help them see who you are. Be careful not to go into TMI territory though! (See the EssaySnark blahg at http://essaysnark.com/2010/11/tmi-or-not-tmi-more-on-evaluating.html for some guidance on what might be considered "TMI" in bschool essays.) If you go down this path, then you must focus on *what you did* in order to really fit the question. Just talking about some bad thing that happened isn't giving us any insight into who you are as a person; you'd need to take the opportunity to fully explore how you changed as a result, and what you did in response, etc.

- If your quantitative skills are not self-evident through the other parts of your application – in other words, if you scored lower than a 46 or so on the quant side of the GMAT, or if you ever had a C or worse in a quant subject in college, and if you're not working in an obviously analytical field – then one way to counter that is to feature one story that has a quant edge to it. If you can find a way to highlight a professional project where you built a model, developed the budget, or even ran some type of analytics on something, then that can add value – but please don't choose such a story only because it's got a quant edge, if it's not the strongest story to offer. If you can expound on those quant skills, then the example must be specific in terms of how you describe what you did. When done right, this type of multi-dimensional approach can add a lot of value for the adcom in better understanding your capabilities even with a limited amount of essay real estate.

- Generally speaking, unless you are heavily involved in the community with a long track record of participation in volunteer work or what have you, we would not suggest featuring a story about extracurriculars as support for something you're pitching in this essay. What we mean is, if the extent of your volunteer work happens on one weekend per year, or you don't have any significant volunteer work to speak of since you graduated from college, then we don't recommend layering that stuff in with this essay. You can still talk about how you want to do some community service as part of your Duke experience but that probably should not be the main attraction of this essay. You just wouldn't have enough credible background info to support it. If this is you, then whatever volunteer experience you do have can be sufficiently captured on the resume and in the application dataset; you don't need to stretch to make it more than it is for the purposes of this essay.

- That being said, if you have an important experience to relate in Essay 2 that comes from the domain of your community service activities or team sports, then great, definitely include it. You can link up such references to the activities you're saying you want to get involved with at Duke. Travel and marathons are pretty typical topics for bschool essays, though that doesn't mean they're off limits for you. Just be sure to connect the dots from whatever you present as your past experiences, to the things you say you will contribute to as a Fuqua student.

- Remember to keep the focus on *leadership*. It's part of the question that they've asked, and using a story or two to back up the implicit assertion that you have good leadership experience going on in your background already – this is important.

## Think about it this way

If a graduating student is going to be recognized for something, there's always a reason for WHY. If you say that you would be recognized as the one who most exemplified a specific Principle, then it's the ACTIONS that you made that got you that recognition.

So your essay needs to focus on what you want to do while at Fuqua. It's not enough just to say you're interested in such-and-such opportunity. How will you do something unique and different? How will your contribution take the Fuqua community to a new place?

This clearly requires some research on your part. We're betting that the Duke student club presidents will be inundated this season with Brave Supplicants wanting to grill them for what they've been doing and what new ideas they have. Hopefully you're coming at this early enough in the season that they won't be sick and tired of fielding such inquiries, and will be motivated to share some fresh information with you! Otherwise you may end up reciting in your essays the same things that that club president has told dozens of other applicants. There's nothing wrong with that, necessarily, but you will also want to incorporate your own thinking and ideas into what you talk about.

This essay is actually quite straightforward to write:

1. State the Principle

2. Explain what you plan to do that would get you recognized for an award for exhibiting that Principle.

3. Reference something from your past that shows how this is a realistic and feasible thing for you to be doing. Give your on-campus aspirations some context.

Your reference to which Principle you're demonstrating can come at the beginning – often recommended, since it sets the stage for your reader and you will avoid losing her in confusion as you go. But this technique is admittedly a little clunky. It can still work though – in fact, you can try rephrasing the essay question as your lead-in to the essay: "If I were to receive an award at the end of my two years at Fuqua, I think it would be..." There's nothing wrong with this very straightforward approach to opening (in your own words, of course!).

Warning: How you talk about this intended future award is tricky. The phrasing of this can be very awkward, since you're both talking about a hypothetical situation in some unrealized future time, and also because it forces you to brag about yourself in a way, which can come across as very unappealing. You will likely need to do multiple revisions on this part, to get the balance down well.

Well. We told you that the second option for Essay 2 was tougher to write. You'll need to do the same type of outreach to the school for either version you choose for Essay 2, but you need to do a lot more strategizing for how to present it in this alternate prompt. Which to us means that that's a great one to do! It will be harder to do a good job with this question, but when you do, oh boy will you stand out from the crowd.

## The Optional Essay

The optional essay for Duke is limited only to conveying as-yet-unexplained and very important details about your candidacy that you cannot capture in the main essays.

There's only a few categories of topics that deserve to be covered in the Duke optional essay. This isn't meant as an essay you can include if you just want to share more stuff with the adcom. You have plenty of space for that in Essay 1 and Essay 2. Appropriate topics for the Optional Essay include, as some possibilities, explaining why you're not getting a recommendation from your current boss, or telling the adcom what you were doing during the time shown as a gap on your resume. Or, the optional essay can be used to give them additional context around your college experience to help them understand why your grades weren't so good. It's not a place to blabber on about more stories and stuff that you wanted to include in the main essays but couldn't.

Do not be tempted to write the optional essay for anything other than problems or weaknesses in your application that cannot be otherwise explained.

Just like with every school in the world (MIT Sloan being one exception), the optional essay should only be used if it's *needed* – not just because it's available. Don't try to color outside the lines. Stick to the main essays, do a great job with those, and only deploy the optional essay for Duke (or any school) if it's absolutely necessary to give the adcom new information that they will need to understand your candidacy.

If you do have something critical to convey, the write it out clearly, and do it briefly. Most people can do so in only 250 words or so.

It's fine to cover multiple topics in the optional essay if needed – hopefully you don't have that many weaknesses to explain, but sometimes there are, well, issues. Just be brief on everything.

Also, sorry to punt on this but in terms of the reapplicant essay: You need to get the *Reapplicant Guide* for how to prepare appropriately. We'd be doing you a disservice to try and cram in a page or so on a reapp essay here. It needs to be a reapp strategy. Hopefully you've got that book already and you're ahead of the game with it.

## What to Do Next

You need to do some homework! And send some emails, make some phone calls, plan your trip. All that fun stuff. We wish you speed and inspiration as you get you moving towards a happy set of essays for Fuqua!

This year's essays are fair. They're welcoming. The Fuqua adcom is always interested in truly learning about you. Hold up your part of the bargain by putting in the effort – and doing some of these brainstorming exercises, and giving yourself enough time to let the best ideas percolate up to the surface of your mind before you start cranking out some half-baked drafts – and you are likely to see a very positive outcome here.

We're happy to field questions through the comments feature on our website, and we've also got some Duke essay reviews up on our site; we did several covering last year's Duke essays on GMAT Club as well.

If you're game for getting your Duke essay reviewed publicly for free – particularly Essay 2 Option 2 – then please hit us up (click the Contact link on essaysnark.com for submission instructions). Or if we can help in any other way, please don't hesitate to reach out – try us on Twitter http://twitter.com/essaysnark if we can offer quick tips or advice about the school or your apps, or email the team at gethelpnow@essaysnark.com with questions about our services.

Or find us on Twitter (@EssaySnark) if you want to hit us up directly for some advice on how to handle your Fuqua essays.

Good luck with it!

Look for other *SnarkStrategies Guides* (digital and paperback) at your favorite bookseller or on the EssaySnark blahg.